Chasing Hellhounds

Also by Marvin Hoffman

Vermont Diary

The Whole Word Catalog
  with Rosellen Brown, Martin Kushner,
  and Sheila Murphy

Chasing Hellhounds

*A Teacher Learns
from His Students*

Marvin Hoffman

MILKWEED
EDITIONS

Published 1996 by Milkweed Editions
Printed in the United States of America
Cover art and design by Sally Wagner
Interior design by Will Powers
The text of this book is set in ITC Slimbach.
96 97 98 99 00   5 4 3 2 1
First Edition

The epigraph on page xiii is from August Wilson,
Fences (New York: Penguin, 1986).

Milkweed Editions is a not-for-profit publisher. We gratefully acknowledge
support from the Bush Foundation; Target Stores, Dayton's, and Mervyn's
by the Dayton Hudson Foundation; Ecolab Foundation; General Mills
Foundation; Honeywell Foundation; Jerome Foundation; The McKnight
Foundation; Andrew W. Mellon Foundation; Kathy Stevens Dougherty and
Michael E. Dougherty Fund of the Minneapolis Foundation; Minnesota State
Arts Board through an appropriation by the Minnesota State Legislature;
Challenge and Literature Programs of the National Endowment for the Arts;
The Ritz Foundation on behalf of Mr. and Mrs. E. J. Phelps Jr.; Piper Jaffray
Companies, Inc.; The Lawrence M. and Elizabeth Ann O'Shaughnessy
Charitable Income Trust in honor of Lawrence M. O'Shaughnessy; John
nd Beverly Rollwagen Fund of the Minneapolis Foundation; The St. Paul
Companies, Inc.; Star Tribune/Cowles Media Foundation; Surdna
Foundation; James R. Thorpe Foundation; Lila Wallace-Reader's Digest
Literary Publishers Marketing Development Program, funded through a grant
to the Council of Literary Magazines and Presses; U. S. West Foundation; and
generous individuals.

Library of Congress Cataloging-in-Publication Data

Hoffman, Marvin, 1939–
    Chasing hellhounds : a teacher learns from his students /
Marvin Hoffman. — 1st ed.
        p.   cm.
    ISBN 1-57131-214-5
    1. High school teaching—United States.   2. Diaries—
Authorship—Study and teaching (Secondary)—United States.
3. Hoffman, Marvin, 1939–   .   4. High school teachers—United
States—Biography.   5. Teacher-student relationships—United
States.   I. Title.
LB1607.5.H64   1996
373.11'02—dc20   96-8264
                                                           CIP

This book is printed on acid-free paper.

To the women in my life—Posey, Adina, and Elana—
who have surrounded me with more love than any man
deserves, and who have assured me that these stories
they have lived and listened to should be heard by others too

Portions of this book have appeared in other forms in *English Journal, Pathways, Holistic Education Review, Teachers and Writers Magazine,* and *The ALAN Review.*

Chasing Hellhounds

Introduction

I have been a public school teacher for more than twenty years. So much has faded, become silted over by the extraordinarily rich sediment of the intervening years. Last week in the post office I met a student from my early teaching days. She is about to graduate from college. We spent her fifth and sixth grade years together in the basement of a tiny New Hampshire mill town school. She was one of the deepest, most sensitive, most talented people I have ever worked with—a favorite in a business where favorites are verboten. "Those were very special years," she said after we had embraced. I nodded agreement, but I wanted to shout, "Jennifer, tell me how they were special. Restore the faded memories." I wanted to be like Emily in *Our Town,* who after her death pleads for the opportunity to relive just one day of her disappeared life in all its sensual detail. Then I could show you what it feels like, tastes like, smells like, to be a teacher, to be close to children's lives for six hours a day, 180 days a year.

My wife sits at home writing novels, but when I unload on her all my tales of triumph and tragedy, humor and sadness, she tells me that I live a novel every day. So do all teachers, if they choose to read their experience that way, and it's time for us to start sharing more of the chapters with one another, as well as with parents and all lovers of the literature of life. We will remind them and ourselves that teaching is, however uncool the word, a noble profession. A friend once even contended that it is among the few remaining ways to earn an honest living. Perhaps some young people on the cusp of their career choices will read this and discover that gratification might lie elsewhere than in the courtroom, hospital, office, or laboratory. We need you. The kids need you.

Here is the heart of the matter, the students themselves. Not every student I've worked with has invited me into his or her life to the extent that the kids in this book have. For whatever reason, the others have found what they needed to sustain them elsewhere—in their families, in themselves, among their peers. I respect their choices just as I respect the right of my students to shelter the privacy of their personal journals from gratuitous prying.

Those who are represented here demonstrate that we must open ourselves to listening to students' voices, to receiving and accepting who they are and what they care about; we must convince them that their real lives can find a legitimate home in the school curriculum. When that happens they will reward us with the considerable gift of themselves. Behind the pimples and the noise, the quirky clothing and hairdos, the undone assignments and the inappropriately directed sexual energy reside some of the strongest, most admirable people I've met, regardless of age. Just at the moment when I find myself annoyed or irritated with them—no rare occurrence for any teacher—I am reminded of the invisible loads they are shouldering. Some of them sink under that weight, and that is no surprise. The wonder is those who don't. Every one of the students—the people—here embodies a mysterious, faith-restoring resilience.

So, Jennifer, these chapters from my imperfectly recalled living novel are for you—and for Warinda, Katie, Tracy, Joshua, Stephanie, Michael, Gwendolyn, Marissa, Jackie, Marcus, Nijole, Peka, Laura, and all the other young people who have enriched my life in ways that extend far beyond the walls of the classrooms we shared.

Lyons:
What you been doing, Uncle Gabe?

Gabriel:
Oh, I been chasing hellhounds and waiting on the time
to tell St. Peter to open the gates.

Lyons:
You been chasing hellhounds, huh? Well . . . you doing the
right thing, Uncle Gabe. Somebody got to chase them.

Gabriel:
Oh, yeah . . . I know it. The devil's strong. The devil ain't
no pushover. Hellhounds snipping at everybody's heels.
But I got my trumpet waiting on the judgment time.

Fences
AUGUST WILSON

Chasing Hellhounds

PART ONE

Jones: Setting the Stage

CHAPTER 1

The Cast

A high school classroom in Houston, Texas. Every face but mine in this sophomore English class is black or brown. We are seated around odd, kidney-shaped tables arranged in an ellipse so that everyone in the room can see everyone else's face. On a table near the front blackboard, I have spread out my grade book, a pile of papers to be returned, a mimeographed copy of today's revised bell schedule, a copy of *Of Mice and Men* from which I plan to read to the class, and the latest issue of *Sports Illustrated*, which has just arrived for the class library, unlike last week's swimsuit issue, which never quite made it into my box.

I share a table with three students. There is Alma, who has been through at least four major hairdos this year and is currently favoring gilded curls piled high on her head like a ripe bunch of Chiquita bananas. On the mornings when we write in our journals, Alma busies herself in her notebook and is first to volunteer to read her entry. One day she writes about seeing her dead father's ghost; on another it is a pained account of the humiliation she suffered at the hands of a friend on whom she lavished an expensive Christmas gift, only to be given a secondhand sweater in return. Or she recounts an early memory of wetting her pants in school. It is her delivery that, without fail, sets off peals of good-natured laughter around the other tables. Alma half-reads, half-interjects, looking up during the laughter to announce earnestly, "I'm serious." During the embarrassing parts, she covers her pursed lips with a cupped hand in an almost vaudevillian gesture of self-consciousness.

Next to her sits Shretta, a late arrival, one of several transfers from the English class next door where Mrs. Holden, on the edge of retirement, betrays her unconscious racism in her every misstep. She drove another student, Vonda, a lovely, intelligent young woman, into my class by informing her that her provocative style of dress will soon get her pregnant. Shretta is a dark, compact, hard-muscled girl who is one of the mainstays of the girls' basketball team. For weeks she was silent, almost sullen in class, observing the proceedings warily until she decided that there was no price to be paid for coming out of hiding. Now she has proven herself one of the most delightfully mischievous and wry-humored members of the class, and we all look forward to her unmaliciously sarcastic interjections during my instructions or my comments about a story we are reading together.

My final tablemate is James, an overweight young man with handsome features who is brave enough to choose the seat at my elbow, the one that every student eschews in the quest for safe distance from the teacher. Every day when he enters, he scans the table to see if the new *Sports Illustrated* has arrived and immediately arranges to check it out overnight. I began leaving *SI* out as bait for James, once I discovered that we shared a passionate interest in basketball (not as passionate as that of La Shanda, at the next table, whose journal is filled with entries rehearsing her intentions to marry Michael Jordan). James is lazy; he puts himself out

very little for most classroom assignments, but when he decided I was allowing students to write about what they really
know and care about, he began to produce a stream of sports
journalism and commentary that revealed a keen eye and a
budding style.

The work was good enough that, in a fit of messianic
zeal, I called an editor friend at the *Houston Chronicle*, told
him about James, and asked for advice about how to capital-
ize on James's interest. A few weeks later we were touring
the paper together, having lunch with my friend and a special features writer who was a former athlete himself. Both
men discussed summer job possibilities with James, but,
unfortunately, James's derelictions bought him a date with
summer school and the job never materialized.

From the perch of my raised, blue-cushioned stool, I scan
the sea of faces around the room. There is Detra, straight-
backed, chocolate-skinned, hair cropped close to the skull.
On designated days, she wears her starched, pressed, im-
maculate Jones ROTC uniform to school.

"Dr. H, my goal is to make a ninety-five in your class,"
she announced to me on our first day together.

"I'll be rooting for you, Detra," I replied, delighted by this
expression of ambition so at odds with the more typical willingness to make do with a seventy, anything that will move
you along on the conveyor belt to nowhere.

Detra was a natural-born teacher. She approached each
oral presentation as a pedagogical challenge and always
managed to hit upon a device that drew her audience in.

"How many y'all don't live with your mamas and
daddies? How many y'all don't even know your daddies?"
This was her opening gambit in a characteristically theatrical
presentation of the book she had read, a novel about a girl
who lived with her grandmother.

Students were willing to respond to personal probes like

these from Detra because she had been so open about her own devastating story in the journals she chose to read to us. Back in Ohio, her crack-addicted mother had threatened to kill her several times and had been trading her daughter's eleven-year-old body for drugs. To save herself, Detra located her father in Houston and arranged to live with the man she hardly knew. In the ultimate betrayal, he raped her, and she was removed to a foster home that, while it lacked warmth and emotional support, at least offered safety and stability. Detra's picture and story had appeared in a piece about foster care in a local newspaper supplement, and she was active in a school support group for abuse victims. Although I was dazzled by this valiant young woman's resilience in the face of her crushing history, even for Detra, the dark clouds descended from time to time. "I'm human, too. Sometimes I get down about all that's happened to me, but I want to help other girls going through what I did, 'cause I sure didn't have no one to turn to."

In the spring of our year together, Detra's class made a series of trips to a local museum—a first for most of them— where they were asked to fix on a particular object that compelled them in some mysterious way. As I wandered through the galleries, checking on the students' progress, I came upon Detra, pad in hand, sprawled in front of a sculpture by John Chamberlain, a colorful, jagged-edged construction fashioned from the body parts of wrecked cars. The piece had elicited snickers of contempt from the group when we made our introductory pass through the galleries. I knelt beside her. "What do you like about it, Detra?"

"You know that Transformers show on TV that little kids like to watch? It's kinda like that. He's transformed this junk into something interesting to look at so you forget what it's made of."

And that's Detra. Endowed with an extraordinary gift of

resilience, she has managed to rise from the wreckage of her life determined to become, in spite of everything that has been done to her, something beautiful for the world—and for herself—to behold.

Next to Detra sits Ernesto. As she recounts her personal horror stories in a disconcertingly businesslike tone, he listens with a bemused look, still apparently unconvinced that such revelation can be made safely in a classroom. Ernesto is a handsome, thickly built young man with classic Mayan features: jet-black straight hair, sculpted nose, the square face of a piece of temple sculpture.

Ernesto is the first to pick up on the subtleties of the reading we do together. I see his head nodding to signal comprehension and agreement when I remark that George's killing of Lenny at the end of *Of Mice and Men* is an act of love. Ernesto had come to our school's Vanguard magnet program for the gifted, but had left for a year and was placed in the regular program for neighborhood kids when he returned.

That is the outer layer of the onion, what Ernesto revealed in his journals and in our whispered conferences conducted while the class was engaged in a writing project or in the astonishingly absorbing independent reading periods I scheduled weekly when students not usually considered avid readers became completely engrossed in books of their own choice.

Ernesto had left Jones High School because the strain between him and his stepfather had grown too great to bear. The atmosphere was so tense at home that Ernesto was depressed about the prospect of having to spend the late-evening hours between his job and bedtime in the strife-torn apartment. Where could he hang out safely in those odd, in-between hours? In desperation, I loaned Ernesto my card for the Rice University library, where I knew he would be safe until as late as one in the morning, and where he could bring his beloved little portable typewriter to a remote place in the stacks and clatter away undisturbed.

Eventually he had no choice but to leave home and move in with a relative in another part of town. During that year, in a different school, Ernesto started doing cocaine, and it was only through dogged monitoring by a devoted cousin—himself a nonusing drug dealer—that he was able to quit after six hellish months.

Now he was back home for another try, confiding to me that he was terrified by the ghostly visits his cravings paid him. When he got the shakes, he was sure he was on his way back down and, truth to tell, I wasn't always sure whether he was being straight with me about whether we were situated before or after the fall.

In Ernesto's case, his ordeal was not for public consumption by his classmates, although it surfaced obliquely in his reactions to the reading we were doing together. His struggles with his stepfather made him particularly sensitive to the thundering tyranny that Troy Maxson attempted to impose on his son Cory in August Wilson's *Fences*, or to Frederick Douglass's struggles with his vicious overseers. Ernesto's brooding pain was a constant presence in our classroom, though his classmates were unaware of its source.

Alma, Shretta, James, Detra, Ernesto, and I are six of twenty-four inhabitants of a very typical American urban ghetto high school classroom. The surrounding neighborhood hides its vices behind a facade of small cottages. The neatly dressed students in this sophomore class are the survivors; a fair number of their classmates have already dropped out, disappeared from the school roll. Two of the girls in the class are already mothers and two others are pregnant.

But that is all immaterial to what actually goes on in this classroom. By their own testimony, Alma and company are different here than in most of their other classes; they are closer to being themselves. They laugh, at times they act silly, they come out of their carefully constructed school masks. The reason for the difference in their behavior is embarrassingly simple. I have tried to construct an environment in which students are more in control of their activities. I do not tell them where to sit. I do not insist on the topics they are to write about in their journals, nor do I even insist on reading what they reveal to their journals. They have frequent opportunities to choose their own reading, as well as the topics they will pursue in long-term writing projects. When we discuss the literature we are reading, the students often formulate the questions we will address, rather than responding to my agenda. Many of the projects we tackle in my class are collaborations in which they and their fellow group members must make important decisions together, negotiate differences, and bear responsibility for the final product. Earlier in the semester, Alma, Shretta, and James created a giant Paper Person—a life-size figure drawn on butcher paper from James's body outline after he had lain on the paper and allowed the others to sketch his outline. Together they endowed him with a personality and a life history and created encounters between him and the other Paper People who were rising, Frankenstein-like, from the sheets of the other groups.

In some of my other classes, the students even formulate their own examination questions. And always, everyone is producing written evaluations of our work, as well as self-evaluations of their own performance and growth.

None of this is particularly innovative. The educational journals are filled with examples of English classrooms designed to produce a more active engagement with reading and writing. It all seems so simple and clear to those of us who do it. In any setting, if you give people responsibility, show you respect them, give them some control over the decisions that affect them, they will perform at their best, far better than if they are simply instructed and then set to work in a highly controlled environment.

Yet the prevailing practice remains otherwise in most institutions. Witness the following statement from *Inside Grade 8: From Apathy to Excitement,* a recent report published by the National Association of Secondary School Principals:

> While many teachers may be sensitive to their students' needs . . . we still found that most eighth graders spent their day as passive learners—listening to teachers, copying from chalkboards, reading assignments, filling in worksheets and taking tests.
>
> To remedy the problem . . . the structure of the 8th grade learning environment should be revamped to give students the opportunity to participate, question, choose options and exercise responsibility.

Substitute any number for grade eight. The picture will change little. Most students spend their school hours, days, years in highly controlled environments. They are expected to produce in ways defined and policed by others much as they would be on a factory assembly line. Even in industry, this model is increasingly discredited. A friend who manages a chemical plant on the polluted rim of industrial Houston has turned over much of the factory's control to his employees, including even the power to hire and fire their co-workers. The result has been greater productivity, lower turnover, and increased job satisfaction. Why are schools so often at the tail end of the parade, ready to move only after the head of the line is already out of sight?

Children come to us out of the most authoritarian of all institutions—the family. Few of them are fortunate enough to grow up where they are permitted to make serious choices or even to participate in important family decisions. Many come to school from families so chaotic as to preclude rational choice and decision making. These children are in even greater need of the skills to assert control over the forces that buffet them like paper boats in a gale. School must be the training ground where a new model is presented, one in which students take responsibility for their own learning in ways that will outlast their school years.

CHAPTER 2

The Setting

As usual, there is only one gate open to the parking lot, which means a drive around the circumference of the school's block-square plot. Even this gate is supposed to be closed after classes begin, but the security guard gets tired of locking and unlocking it for delivery trucks, latecomers, and other strays, so he lets it swing loose.

A quick look around the perimeter of the school grounds leaves you wondering at the reason for the siege mentality; all appears tranquil. Along one side of the building runs a slow-moving, unwholesome-looking bayou lying under a skin of algae and white foam; along the other a wide strip of open land, also belonging to the school district, with No Dumping signs posted at frequent intervals—to no avail. Behind this little caricature of a green belt sits a row of modest houses—more like cottages—that are characteristic of the housing throughout the neighborhood. They are reminiscent of the beach bungalows to which my friends' families retreated for the worst weeks of New York's summer season. None of us ever dreamed that anyone could inhabit these flimsy wooden structures year round. Directly across from the school entrance, the homeowner has planted himself a healthy plot of greens and string beans and keeps a flock of chickens. Like many black Houstonians, he probably moved here from Louisiana and has chosen to bring a bit of it with him. Scattered through the neighborhood are big, open lots on which the only human encroachment is a sign announcing the future site of a church whose ambition has not been realized, judging from the height of the weeds and the weathered state of the sign.

In a moment of divine inspiration, some developer or city official hit upon the idea of transforming the area into a giant theme park of sorts by naming every street after some event, figure, or location connected with one of the World Wars, so in the last part of my journey from the freeway to school I cross Iwo Jima, Patton, Dunkirk, St. Lo, Guadalcanal, and others. I once visited a suburban Long Island community in which all the streets had been named after women in the developer's life—Ann, Carol, Linda, and so on—a literal road map of domestic life and its attachments. What prescience the founders of these two communities had demonstrated in choosing the metaphors that defined their histories—the embattled world of South Park and the tranquil, family-focused universe of Syosset.

I remember watching the television footage of the Watts riots in 1965 and being puzzled by the references to this "slum" neighborhood. For us New Yorkers, slums were tenements, poor people stacked in layers of densely populated apartments woven together by rusting fire escapes. But these were single-family homes, white clapboard, shingled roofs. Patches of grassy lawn and the occasional palm tree just didn't seem to be elements of a slum ecosystem.

South Park is like Watts. If you view it through the tinted windows of a limousine, as I saw the wife of former Secretary of State James Baker do once, it doesn't look half bad.

Indeed, every street has its share of neatly painted homes with manicured lawns, newly built carports to shade the treasured family vehicle from the brutal summer sun, and wrought iron fences to protect people and property from incursions that seem unimaginable on this tranquil morning. The cabs of long-distance rigs are parked alongside several houses, and their owners are busy digging postholes, tending to roof leaks, or hosing down the oddly truncated trailerless cabs before they head out for another stretch on the road.

Between these islands of solidity lie the abandoned houses, their doors and windows covered with plywood in a vain attempt to keep the crackheads, derelicts, and scavengers out. House for Sale says one sign: "$500 down. Financing arranged with owner." In front of some of the occupied houses, old mattresses are heaped alongside dead branches and rotting lumber. They have become such a fixture of the landscape that neither the residents nor the sanitation men seem to notice them any longer.

There are no sidewalks in South Park. At the end of the school day, the "walkers"—the neighborhood kids who do not depend on the city or school district buses for transportation—are forced out into the middle of the road where the passing cars must pick their way between them as they pass through the neighborhood. Where the sidewalk might be there are instead drainage ditches intended to carry away the runoff from the frequent thunderstorms that assault this semitropical big city. Any sustained downpour causes the ditches to overflow, turning South Park and many other Houston neighborhoods into lakes better traversed by rowboat than by car.

One rainy morning, there were cars stalled on the streets and feeder roads, and I had to move slowly to ensure that the wake I created and those I encountered from passing cars didn't flooded my engine. I was without brakes most of the

time and had to pick my way through the streets near school
that were least likely to be flooded.

Once the rains came in the last sleepy hours before the
end of the school day, assaulting the windows of my classroom with such vehemence that the treeline across the bayou
lost its outlines in a translucent haze. By dismissal time, we
knew we were in a state of siege. The occasional passing bus
or truck showed water high up on its oversize wheels, and
we knew we weren't going anywhere for some time. Legends
circulated about nights when students and staff were forced
to sleep in the building overnight.

Finally, the rain slowed enough for me to remove my
shoes and socks, wade out to the parking lot, and guess my
way through the least afflicted side streets of South Park,
momentarily washed clean by the flood. I knew that the next
day the banks of the bayou would be clogged with old tires
and plastic detritus flushed out by the floodwaters that had
disappeared as mysteriously as they came.

There are only two businesses within sight of the school.
One is a grocery/convenience store whose heavily barred
windows suggest that behind the neighborhood's midmorning tranquility lie unseen troubles. There's a hint of what
those might be at the other business—an underage equivalent of a roadhouse. Actually, it's nothing more than a shop
where kids congregate for soda and snacks at the end of the
day and at whatever other time they can slip past the porous
security net that is supposed to enclose them during school
hours. Often a patrol car is parked in the lot alongside the
store, a potent reminder that violence is never a stranger
when large numbers of teenagers gather. Gangs have recently
resurfaced and drugs are everywhere.

As I park in the school lot, I can hear the Orwellian
rumble of the principal's voice emanating from the speakers

deployed around the grounds. The effect is eerie. The president of a small Caribbean country is addressing the populace gathered in the capital's town square—but the square is virtually empty and the voice caroms off the buildings and parked cars before drifting away like smoke.

The school building itself is a product of 1950s functional nonarchitecture: two rectangular spaces, each surrounding a grassy courtyard, the first one story high, the second two, with classrooms laid out shotgun style around the perimeter of each. Low-density construction suitable for a low-density city, a sharp contrast to the beehive high-rise schools in New York City that mimic the apartment house/tenement motif of their surroundings.

There are no steps leading up to a front door, no imposing rotunda or lobby to swallow you definitively when you enter. Visitors often stop in puzzlement to ask me where the entrance is and I point to a narrow opening beyond the auto shop and the wood shop, which face out onto the parking lot. Through that gap lies a tunnel-like covered walkway reminiscent of the dark ramps in the major league ballparks of my youth that directed eager fans out into the brilliant sunlight and grassy green vista at the stadium's heart.

At Jones High School, the walkway carries you past a tiny courtyard open to the air on all four sides but sheltered from the relentless Houston sun and the tropical rains by a metal roof. Here, the overflow lunch crowd gathers at picnic tables, and after school squads of young men and women practice their elaborate line dancing routines for the step shows that are major entertainment events for the black students.

No matter what the period or time of day, kids are clustered around the pay phones just inside the front door in noisy conversations with boyfriends, with moms who need to pick them up, with bosses who need to be told why Taco

Bell or Target will have to do without their employees' services today.

Beyond the pay phones stretch unbroken ribbons of locker-lined corridors extending on the long side of the rectangle a full city block. At each crossroads stand building administrators checking students' passes to determine the legitimacy of their right to be away from class.

"I just need to get something from my locker."

"You do that before or after class, young lady."

"But I need something for my book report."

"You should have thought of that before. Now turn right around and go back where you came from, and don't let me see you out here again. Haven't we had this conversation before?"

It is the unchanging school ballet—order and authority aligned against limit testing and restlessness.

For the most part, order is winning at Jones. The halls are relatively clear when classes are in session, free of both people and refuse as the ubiquitous janitorial crew sweeps the halls with imposing corridor-width dust mops, capturing in their wake stray candy wrappers, crumpled assignments, and whatever else may have fallen from a hastily ransacked locker. The building, anchored at one end by an auditorium and library and at the other by two gyms and a pool, is in relatively good repair. Some recent renovations, supported by a citywide bond issue, carpeted several classrooms, including mine, improved the science lab, and touched up other minor structural and cosmetic shortcomings. The courtyard, where many of the students eat, flirt, and toss Frisbees at lunch, has been landscaped and equipped with stone benches, although most of the kids still prefer to sprawl out on the uncomfortable stone walkways.

It's a functional environment, unremarkable, unstimulating, and, behind the orderly facade, ill equipped for serious learning. Computers are just now beginning to appear in the building, their numbers still hardly up to the task of serving the school's thirteen hundred-odd students. The library was a morgue with tables until an energetic, underfunded new librarian took over this year. It will remain totally inadequate for student research for years to come, although a computer link with the Rice University library gives Jones students at least an invitation to get their toes wet as the Tofflers' Third Wave rolls ashore.

Apart from the unaccountable touch of carpeting, my room resembles most of the others. A bank of windows faces either the street or the courtyard, bringing a steady supply of sunlight through grimy, unwashed windows. Mine looks out on the refuse-clogged bayou; sometimes a graceful, snowy white egret sets down on the uninviting banks and I am drawn from my work to gape at this apparition.

The slab walls are cold and unwelcoming to all forms of adhesive; student work and posters are rejected like incompatible organ transplants. I've attempted to soften the surroundings with plants and with Mexican blankets thrown across tables and file cabinets as if they were ponies prepared to be mounted. A few teachers have opted for tables rather than the familiar chairs with armrests sprouting from their sides. Although these chairs can be arrayed in creative ways to enable group work, the tables signal a more democratic participatory milieu in which students are encouraged to attend to each other rather than spending another mind-numbing period being addressed by the teacher.

Every available space around the circumference of my room is lined with bookshelves scavenged from classrooms and storerooms where they sat unused. Even if the school library were more inviting, I've learned that it's easier to encourage students to read when the books are right up in their faces where I can entice them with engaging titles. The books are a motley collection of yard sale castoffs, second-hand bookstore purchases, and reviewer's copies from a local newspaper for which I do a monthly column. Every year, a certain percentage of the collection walks out from under my porous record-keeping system, but I console myself with visions of these books on bedside tables or sharing valuable shelf space with Al Green and Boyz II Men.

This year the school jettisoned the old fifty-minute-period schedule and replaced it with the currently fashionable block scheduling—ninety-minute classes that meet every other day rather than daily. Now a student's day consists of three course blocks, with an hour-long lunch period separating the second and third. At first, many students and teachers were nervous about the impending shift.

Student: "How am I going to stay awake in that teacher's class for an hour and a half when I'm dying in there now for fifty minutes?"

Teacher: "How am I going to maintain discipline for that long when the class has such a limited attention span even now?"

But, in fact, some teachers have gotten the message that if they stop talking at kids for a full period and try instead to vary their activities, the time is, if anything, too short. Students have discovered that there are virtues to seeing their most boring teachers only every other day. A bit of variety helps the sometimes unpalatable school day go down more easily, and half as many hall passings and attendance takings decrease the fragmentary, frenetic qualities of the school day.

Jones is really two schools in one. Roughly 80 percent of the students are neighborhood kids zoned to the school solely on the basis of residence. The other 20 percent have chosen to be bused to Jones from all over the city to be part of a magnet program for gifted and talented students called

Vanguard. When I first came to Jones seven years ago, almost all the neighborhood kids were black. In a school system where less than 15 percent of the students are white, integration is an empty term. Most Houston schools are pre- dominantly either black or Hispanic. In the context of our school, integration comes in two forms. In the "regular" pro- gram, little clusters of Hispanic and Vietnamese students have sprouted like wildflowers. They traverse the hallways together, chattering in their native languages, still very much visitors on someone else's turf, but with enough critical mass to begin to be a presence.

Integration in the more traditional sense exists only in the Vanguard program, where 25 percent of the students are white. The magnet program was originally designed as an alternative to forced busing, and to the extent that the gener- ally limited supply of whites allows, it has worked. If you see a white face at Jones, it belongs to a Vanguard student, drawn by the quality of the academic program.

Jones isn't an easy sell to parents of any race who have other options, given the neighborhood's reputation for vio- lence and drugs.

But the truth is that even allowing for the naiveté and blinders of teachers like me, there aren't a lot of drugs in the building. Most of it has remained on those quiet-looking streets. The marketplace of consumers and providers is com- posed of people who have found more congenial turf than the school on which to perform their death dances. In fact, for many kids, the school is a city of refuge, a safe haven from the world of drugs. Last year when Kenya arrived in my class in midyear, I asked him to write me a letter of introduction:

> My life style is not like 16 year olds. Because I live in the
> fast lane. Going out to nightclubs such as the Rhinestone,
> the Benny and other clubs. But I hang with 21 and 23 year
> old men. I was a drug dealer selling crack, but it's not

worth it. Your making money but you're killing people. I
drink every now and then. But I don't like the fast life style.
Because you're going to wind up dead or in jail and I don't
want neither one. Like when I was selling crack I was making 7 to 15 hundred dollars a week, 2 and 3 hundred a day.
But since someone killed my best friend February 22, 1989
and threw him in a ditch I didn't like that not one bit. I
don't sell nothing any more that's not how I want to end
up. So I figured I'll go to school and graduate because I
want to be an actor.

Who knows how long Kenya will stay, now that he's
come in from the cold, but the point is that he sees the
school as a safety zone, a place where the drug dogs sent to
sniff out forbidden substances in student lockers are going
to come up empty, save for a few ripening peanut butter and
jelly sandwiches. This security comes at a price. The halls
and grounds are regularly patrolled by two officers from the
Houston Police Department, a plainclothes school district
security guard who scans the parking lot and entrances from
his perch outside the auto mechanics shop, and the "substance abuse monitor" (SAM), a nattily dressed gentleman
who struts through our halls, walkie-talkie in hand, our permanent drug dog in residence.

At times, when I go by the office of the assistant principal, the catch basin for all disciplinary action, I witness kids
being frisked by cops or simply being glared into silence.
These kids are likely to evaporate from the school. Their
names will appear on tomorrow's attendance list under "sus-
pended" and the campus peace will be preserved. The price
here is the violation of student rights and the larger price
we all pay for dumping more undereducated, underprepared,
and angry people outside those school gates.

I have never felt unsafe or threatened in my years at the
school. It is true that several years ago a well-publicized

murder was committed inside the building, but it was an act of domestic violence without any particular threat to outsiders, although it pointed up the existence of an arsenal of hidden weapons, ready to be pressed into action when the emotional temperature rises. A young man ragged on a female classmate in homeroom about the authenticity of her new leather miniskirt. She pulled a hunting knife from her backpack and pursued him into the hall, where she plunged it into his back. He raced down the hall before he collapsed and died in the arms of the assistant principal, who was distraught for days.

The murder was a front-page story that didn't do much to bolster the already difficult efforts to recruit students from other parts of the city for our magnet program. But its effect on daily life in the school was minimal and short-lived—no more representative of daily life at Jones than the killing of a student by her roommate at Harvard represents the daily reality of that institution. After a day or two of tears and the kind of crisis counseling that has become obligatory after suicides, tornadoes, and other natural and unnatural disasters, we were back to what passes for normal throughout the building, an odd mixture of serious learning and some equally serious hanging out—in the overcrowded cafeteria (which I have entered at my own peril only twice in seven years), in the grassy inner courtyard, and around the pay phones.

Jones is a microcosm of the promise and failure of American education. Daily, my teaching load straddles two worlds. When the passing bell rings, I am transported from Westchester to East St. Louis. The kids in both worlds—Vanguard and regular—need me, and I in return rely on them to remind me daily of our responsibility to close the senseless gap between those who are tracked for success and those who are heading nowhere.

If you chanced to enter my Vanguard classroom, you would hear Kate describing her video project, for which she is interviewing people about their conceptions of beauty, where Seth is writing a short story inspired by his reading of Donald Barthelme, where small groups are seated around their rectangular tables discussing the mythic town of Macondo brought to life by Gabriel García Márquez in *One Hundred Years of Solitude*.

Next period these same tables will be occupied by students who have never heard of Hiroshima, who can identify neither the combatants in the Vietnam War nor its outcome. Many of them have reached the tenth grade without having read a single complete novel.

These students may be ignorant, through no fault of their own, but they are not unintelligent. They are often ill prepared, and little has been expected of them, but there is LaShonda, as bright and hungry as any of my Vanguard students; and Vonda, a beautiful young woman and a closet poet who exchanged verses with her boyfriend in jail and who has inhaled my offerings of Maya Angelou, Lucille Clifton, and Alice Walker; and Terence, who overwhelmed us all with his portrayal of Troy Maxson in a scene from August Wilson's *Fences*.

Lord, how do I keep these students moving without discouraging them completely when I tell them how far behind they are already, how hard they will have to work to even catch sight of the heels of the Vanguard students? They don't know what it means to really dig in and work hard in school. No one has ever asked them to. For many, no one has ever stressed how important it is simply to be there every day. Tomorrow is Friday and half of them will be absent, already embarked on an early weekend, and I will be thrown back on my ingenious but ultimately futile devices to keep things moving forward without losing completely the inevitable absentees.

By most standards, Jones is not a successful school. Too many dropouts, too many failures, not enough college-bound students, particularly when the magnet school students, the jewels in the school's crown, are factored out of the equation. Morale is low. The extracurricular glue that binds otherwise mediocre institutions does not exist here. For years there has been no schoolwide newspaper, yearbook, or drama program. The football and basketball teams rarely rise above the middle of the division standings, their work made more difficult by a dwindling student population that has left Jones just one-third the size of the largest school in the league.

When the scores on the statewide academic performance tests are released, the air is filled with accusations and recriminations. For months preceding the tests, there have been workshops, in-service days, packets of study materials, motivational banners and posters in the hall, contests in the auditorium, loudspeaker exhortations by the principal—all to no avail. My unhappy sophomores, very few of whom have passed even one of the required three exams in math, reading, and writing, blame their teachers for failing to prepare them adequately. They generously absolve me from the blanket condemnations, but I carry my own guilt for being too cavalier about the testing, expecting that my heavy doses of reading and writing reflect obliquely in the test scores, but no such luck.

The students also blame the counselors for dumping them into dead-end courses like informal geometry and business math, which prepare them for nothing. When Jennise showed me her schedule, I was shocked to discover the number of filler courses she was taking. "I tried to talk to them about it, but they won't listen to no student. If I had the kind of parents that would come in and fight for me, I wouldn't have a schedule that looks like this." I remembered the encounters, sure as the seasons, with my daughter's high school counselors who had once again produced an unacceptable schedule for her. Jennise could not expect the same from her overburdened parents, and she joined ranks with her teachers and the school administration in pinning the blame on families for undervaluing education and failing to provide the encouragement and atmosphere to produce academic success. To complete the circle, teachers and administrators blamed each other for not fulfilling their professional duties, for expecting too much, and so on. And everyone blames the students for not caring, not trying hard enough, not recognizing the implications of the testing for their futures. In the losing team's locker rooms, finger pointing escalates and accusations are made with just enough truth to cut to the quick.

It should be dispiriting, as are the accounts of the "state of our schools" that appear in educational reports and op-ed columns—and some days it is. But there's too much life and energy here that can't be overlooked. Kids determined to graduate despite pregnancies, despite forty-hour-per-week jobs, because of devoted parents. Kids who want to be judges because they've seen the respect a judge receives when she enters the courtroom. Kids who want to be investment bankers so they can bring money back to the community. Kids who want to be pharmacists so they can buy a house and raise a family.

And teachers and administrators who are bucking the existential odds, investing huge amounts of time in tutoring and counseling, engaging in that enormous uphill struggle to cut the casualties by an important few, while the many continue to fail.

And yet it's hard to resist the spectacle of outrageous

hairdos—boys in their angled flattops or "dos" that make them look like cartoon characters undergoing a thousand-volt electric shock; girls with gilded curls spilling off their heads in every conceivable direction—gold chains, pants with one striped and one polka-dotted leg. It's all part of the ongoing adolescent mating dance.

As I emerge from the building at the end of a school day and head across the parking lot, I adjust my flip-down shades against the glare of the brutal Houston sun. I won't be able to grip the steering wheel today without a cloth to shield my hands from the heat the plastic has been storing all these hours. In the distance I can hear a low bass rumble from the stereos of the students' cars that circle the building every afternoon, their sound turned up to flood the neighborhood with the latest in rap. On the playing field, our chronically losing football team is already out doing laps, prisoners of the same insupportable mixture of hopefulness and despair that plagues both parties in the educational exchange.

I turn the corner, cross the bayou, wave good-bye to a few familiar faces, and head home.

PART TWO

Rehearsals

CHAPTER 3

Derailed by History

Once, when I was applying for a teaching job in a small
rural school in Vermont, the head of the local school committee scanned my résumé, came upon my Harvard Ph.D.,
and asked incredulously, "Are you running away from a
murder rap?"

Our improbable paths to the present go a long way toward
explaining who we are and what we believe. Somewhere
on the road from Mississippi to New York to Vermont to New
Hampshire I discovered the things about kids, about communities, and about learning that give shape to my classroom
in Jones High School, Houston, Texas, where I arrive every
day with both an anticipatory pleasure and a heavy sense of
doubt about whether I'm up to the responsibility.

What I've come to know about children's resilience in
the face of crushing circumstances, about the interconnect-
edness of the school and the community in which it is embedded, about the need for students' learning to be linked
to the lives they live outside the classroom—all this is part
of my personal story. I am one of hundreds of thousands of
teachers in America. My story deserves telling only insofar

as it manages to convey to my colleagues, to parents, to other interested citizens how desperately important the daily dramas are to determining whether this is a country we and our children will be able to inhabit civilly in the future.

My earliest foray into teaching and working with kids came at age nineteen. I was in Israel, an early pioneer in the now fashionable "time out" movement that makes a year abroad during college almost mandatory. I had obediently plodded my way through a freshman year of pre-engineering studies at the City College of New York, knowing all along that it was shriveling my soul. But as a good and compliant son and student, I was not adept at beating my own path through the thicket of choices the world offered. A year abroad was a safe and legitimate way to halt the forced march to an undesired destination.

After six months of study in Jerusalem and two months of kibbutz life, I was assigned to teach school in a newly settled farming village in the northern Negev established to accommodate the staggering influx of new immigrants from the North African and Arab countries.

The students in my school came from two adjacent villages. Some of us made the same walk twice daily across as yet uncultivated fields to a new and charmless cinder block structure that had not been designed so much as imposed upon the barren hillside where it stood. The children originally came from one of three places: Djerba, an island off the coast of Tunisia that had been host to an ancient and proud Jewish community; Spanish Morocco, a slice of old colonialist territorial spoils that produced young children capable of speaking French, Spanish, Arabic, and now Hebrew—a living reproach to those of us struggling with only our second language; and Casablanca, where the children's families saw themselves as far more sophisticated and worldly than their rural neighbors.

I taught alongside young army recruits, women assigned to noncombat roles in an army in which everyone, regardless of sex, serves. None of us knew a thing about teaching, nor did we receive any guidance or training. Night after night I read the soft-covered history text in a frantic effort to keep a step ahead of my students, uncertain that my newly acquired Hebrew was up to comprehending the material. I wondered what to do with the text other than repeating it in my own words or having students read it aloud in class.

Either way, I wasn't able to wrestle much attention from my students, possessed as they were of the energy and restlessness appropriate to their age, compounded by an uncanny ability to exploit every weakness of a frightened teenager. That meant resorting to disciplinary measures, about which I had not the slightest idea. Corporal punishment? Heads on the desks? A spell of standing in the corner? In the orderly and compliant world in which I grew up, I had seen very little discipline meted out. My only models were pale replicas of nineteenth-century schoolhouse practice, reflected dimly through films and books. In any case, I was bad at it: the kids knew it as well as I did, and that accelerated the downhill slide. Some days the din rising from the multilingual Babel was unbearable. They reached down to hidden places in their throats to produce sounds that came naturally to a speaker of Arabic but were out of reach of my Brooklyn English.

When I left the village to return to Jerusalem, it was hardly with the sense that I had found my mission in life. I was not to become a teacher of young children for another fourteen years.

When I returned to college in New York, I put aside my engineering studies in favor of psychology. From CCNY to graduate school at Harvard, I seemed headed for a traditional clinician's office, complete with laminated diplomas for my patients to admire. I never spent a day in that mythical office, never practiced the profession in any way Dr. Freud would recognize.

History in the form of the civil rights movement derailed me. As the sit-ins, freedom rides, demonstrations, and marches became the stuff of the nightly news, I was growing increasingly restless and guilty about my safe, disengaged student life, even though it included what proved to be a very formative year as a teaching assistant in an extraordinarily popular and well attended race relations course.

As soon as my dissertation work was done, my wife and I left for Mississippi to teach at Tougaloo, a predominantly black college on the northern edge of Jackson, the state capital, the last promontory on the shore of a rural ocean that stretched unbroken through the Delta until it reached Memphis. Teaching psychology here was to be my modest, circumscribed contribution to the civil rights movement.

Four hours on campus was all it took for us to cast aside the caution that had led us to promise our parents that we would not appear in public in integrated groups. Several students asked if we could drive them to town to see a play called *In White America*, a documentary account of racial oppression. In the act of agreeing to chauffeur these bright, eager young people, we set in motion a process that led us into a deeper engagement and activism than we had envisioned.

If teaching courses on race relations and social psychology seemed uncomfortably detached in Cambridge, here in the heart of Mississippi it would have been akin to lecturing on sports history in a Superbowl huddle.

One Sunday morning, another group of students, valuing us for our car and overlooking our Jewishness, asked us to drive them to town to attend services at a white church that had not come to terms with the fact that blacks might be part of the human brotherhood.

Although each demonstration, each humiliating and potentially dangerous integrated foray into the white-controlled world, filled us with trepidation, we had long since put detachment behind us. We parked a block from the church and strolled through the Sunday-morning silence as our students went off for their rendezvous with apoplectic ushers and congregants who ranged from icy to abusive.

When they were safely back in the car rehashing their experiences and giving shape to the accounts they would repeat endlessly on campus, I noticed that our gas gauge was low. Stopping at a gas station with an integrated car was never a pleasant prospect, but neither was running out of gas on an empty stretch of road with the same cast of characters.

"How y'all doin' today? Like me to fill her up?"

Good fortune had delivered us into the hands of a friendly attendant and we silently offered our thanks.

He disappeared to the rear to unscrew the gas cap.

"Hey, what's this white stuff?"

He was back at the driver's side window, displaying the powder he had collected on his fingers. We knew immediately but waited for him to make the inevitable discovery.

"I do believe it's sugar."

And indeed it was—an old trick that had put many a civil rights worker's car out of commission. Sugar in the gas tank, heat up the engine, coat the cylinder with caramel like a jelly apple, and good-bye engine. Fortunately, we had driven only a few yards and the harm could be reversed by draining the gas tank and flushing the system.

Experiences like these were the daily lessons in a curriculum that did not honor artificial boundaries between the classroom and the complex, strife-filled world outside.

There was a period in the mid-1960s when Mississippi was as much a magnet for people of prominence as, say, Aspen is today. Artists, writers, lawyers, and scientists converged on the state for stays that lasted anywhere from a single Wednesday to a lifetime. Among these visitors was a group of prominent doctors bearing an interesting proposal to our college's president, who invited me to sit in on the meeting with them.

Dr. G, the leader of the delegation, a doctor with an academic appointment and long list of civil rights bona fides, spoke:

"Mr. O, we've been meeting with a foundation in New York that is willing to put up the seed money for constructing a medical clinic right here on campus. With their endorsement on the project, I'm sure we can raise the remaining money."

Mr. O, a gracious but cautious man, sniffed around this gift box, searching for the hidden explosives. "Lord knows our students could use a better facility. Some of you have seen the conditions Dr. Smith, the campus physician, has to put up with in the infirmary."

"I'm sure your students could benefit greatly from the clinic, but we would also like to make its services available to the people in the community around campus. I'm sure you're more aware than we of how much they need it." Tougaloo, like the black college in Ralph Ellison's *Invisible Man*, was a middle-class island struggling desperately against being drowned by the surrounding sea of poverty. Streets of the village of Tougaloo were still unpaved. Lowering the dike, even though it might bring much-needed water, also brought risks of invasion.

The steam went out of the meeting after the mention of "the community," and although it broke up amidst polite promises to follow up, nothing ever came of the clinic plan.

The experience confirmed for me what I had already begun to intuit about the limits to the college's commitment to acting as a lever for change beyond its boundaries. True, the school had been bold in its willingness to support the civil rights movement and its student leaders so long as the issues being addressed were consonant with the interests of the aspiring middle-class world.

But the problems of poor Mississippians in general, and poor children in particular, were desperate. I had to look beyond the campus for a proper venue for the kind of action that seemed necessary.

It was 1965 and the poverty program was being born in a resource-rich Washington not yet sapped by the burdens of the Vietnam War. In Mississippi, its most visible representative was the Child Development Group of Mississippi (CDGM). This statewide Head Start program was designed and staffed by old civil rights workers and activists from the Mississippi Freedom Democratic Party who saw in it an opportunity to address so many issues of poor children and their families simultaneously—education, health, community, and employment.

CDGM was daring in two respects. First, its activist founders saw education as inextricable from the lives of children and their communities. Children's learning could not be addressed without attending to employment, voter registration, health care, nutrition. At a CDGM parents' meeting in the sanctuary of an unpainted rural church on the edge of a cotton field, the agenda could just as easily deal with proposals for a community water system as with more recognizably "educational" issues. If the children didn't have clean, safe water, they would not be healthy enough to benefit from the most innovative and energetic classroom programs. More than two-thirds of our children were anemic, and on my visits to the centers I often saw them dozing at their tables

as their teachers led the group in singing or while their classmates built towers from the finest set of blocks they had
ever seen.

Second, CDGM was committed to community control
at all levels, from the local centers to the statewide structure.
My job involved overseeing the community organization
efforts aimed at preparing people to exercise that control
effectively. The task was so formidable precisely because the
white leadership of the state had done a surgically perfect
job of eliminating blacks from almost all forms of organizational and institutional life. For a black person in Mayersville,
Mississippi, deep in Delta country, organizational experience
was not likely to extend beyond membership in a church's
board of deacons, where real control lay in the hands of the
pastor in any case and where budgetary decisions seldom
involved figures of more than two or three digits.

CDGM was a program with a budget of six and a half
million dollars and a payroll of more than two thousand
employees. There were entirely unfamiliar issues to be
addressed in a gargantuan organization of this kind: personnel policies, governing structures, budgetary controls, relations with government agencies and organizations, and,
above all, choices of educational approaches and philosophies. Few teachers in the CDGM centers had gone beyond
high school in their own education and many of the parents
were barely literate, yet we were committed to introducing
them to the philosophies and approaches of four or five different preschool education styles so they could decide intel-
ligently how they raised their children to be schooled.

The education of young children was as much new territory for me as for these Mississippi parents as I sat in the
back pews of the rough churches on the edges of cotton
fields and wood lots that housed many of our centers. I listened to the energetic preschool educators on our program

staff enumerating for parents the virtues of block building, of being read aloud to, of providing choice in the day's activities, of finding alternatives to physical punishment. The hardest sell of all was the idea that work sheets and drill might not be the best way for very young children to grow. These parents, many of whom had been cruelly denied the privilege of education, were eager for their children to leapfrog them. They believed in education with a passion sustainable only by those from whom it has been withheld. These gatherings, more like religious meetings than workshops, were the education courses I had never enrolled for, far richer and more meaningful than anything I might have encountered on a college campus.

It was during these sessions, framed by exuberant renditions of "This Little Light of Mine" and "Ain't Gonna Let Nobody Turn Me 'Round," that the classroom was beginning to call to me, as surely as the Holy Spirit was calling my neighbors at these gatherings. Although I had been in and out of scores of Head Start classrooms during my critical years at CDGM, the focus of my work was elsewhere. My arena was primarily political, not pedagogical: gritty community organizers battling the harassment and intimidation of local sheriffs bent on keeping our school buses off the roads or trying to convince local white doctors that it was their Hippocratic responsibility to examine our desperately needy children; indefatigable central office administrators pulling all-nighters to prepare proposals to Washington for refunding or to map political campaigns to keep at bay the segregationist wolves forever threatening to huff and puff and blow our house down.

By the time we finally left CDGM in the hands of the local folks who were its intended trustees all along, I had learned some indelible new lessons about the ways in which education is embedded in a communal context—and a highly politicized bed it often is—but it was still unclear how I would pursue my growing preference for finger paints over politics.

In the fractious political world of the New York City to which we returned in 1968, a monumental battle was being waged between the teachers' union and the minority community over community control of schools. In spite of our desire to stand back and reflect on our intense years in Mississippi before moving off in new directions, that dangerous sense of duty drew us into a fray less life-threatening than that in Mississippi but in many ways more venomous and intractable day to day.

I visited the streets of Ocean Hill-Brownsville in Brooklyn, now a nightmare version of a place I remembered for its sturdy stone apartment buildings. All those buildings were gone, replaced by acres of empty, rubble-strewn lots where small fires smoldered, as if in the aftermath of a bombing.

In a classroom in one of the Ocean Hill elementary schools, the very young children were seated on the floor close to the teacher and her aide. The teacher recited in a clipped, almost military tone, and the children repeated in unison, without variation. This particular method of rote learning was promoted by two educator/psychologists named Bereiter and Engelmann who believed that through group recitation they could lay the bedrock for future learning, an idea that was received well by community parents.

Outside, a picket line of teachers circled the building. The decentralization plan had triggered a strike by the teachers' union, which saw the plan as a threat to its powers to protect teachers from arbitrary dismissal. The faces, distorted with anger, were aimed at every visitor and staff person who crossed the line.

One night we carried our sleeping bags into the elementary school down the street from our brownstone duplex and bedded down in the cafeteria, where we spent the night to ensure that the school would be open for children arriving in the morning against the efforts of the union and the custodians to shut it down. Earlier that day, I had been turned away at the Board of Education, where I had gone to apply for a teaching position to replace the strikers temporarily. I was told that my Harvard Ph.D. did not qualify me to teach children of the city.

It didn't take long for us to recognize that New York was not Mississippi. Ironically, in the country's most backward rural state, change was more possible because many of the institutions of a developed, industrialized economy—unions, layers of local government, entrenched educational bureaucracies—had not yet emerged. Each institution in New York had its own vested interest to protect, its own perceptions of the pitfalls of change. On the other hand, the local groups that were to exercise the new powers had not been the beneficiaries of the years of organizing effort that had been invested in the towns and churches of Mississippi. Even under the best of circumstances, organizing in urban neighborhoods was devilishly more difficult than in small towns and rural areas of the South, where the ties that bind people—kinship, history, and church affiliation—were more palpable.

The result was near disastrous. The local New York groups were vulnerable from within and without. They were not a match for their better-organized foes, who knew how to work the political system to their advantage. Legislation to decentralize the schools was battered into unrecognizability in Albany. The agenda of the demagogues within was the acquisition of power rather than change that would affect children.

This sound political thrashing crystallized my determination to become more directly involved in what happens in the classroom rather than in the proverbial back room. At

that moment, my deus ex machina descended in the form
of an invitation from some former Mississippi colleagues to
direct Teachers and Writers Collaborative, a program that
places writers in classrooms at all grade levels to work with
children and teachers to develop new approaches to teaching writing.

For three years, I watched some wonderful word magi-
cians ignite children's interest in language, instill in them the
realization that words can be pleasurable and powerful, not
the leaded mallets with which they had been bludgeoned
into muteness in their previous classrooms. We published
the students' fanciful creations and the writers' rich diaries.
We begged money for the project and sat with principals to
explain how writing poems in which every line consists of
an outrageous lie might be educationally beneficial to their
children.

Yet the real front lines were elsewhere. I was still rele-
gated to an office with unfinished floors and unwashed windows, lacking only the smell of barbecue and pickled pigs'
feet and the jukebox rumble of Percy Sledge radiating from
below to replicate my Mississippi headquarters. Gloria
Channon, a teacher in East Harlem, was the boatwoman
who finally brought me to the other side. I reviewed a book
about her classroom experiences in a national magazine,
and when she called to thank me, I expressed my frustration
at forever playing the role of educational procurer, with
never a chance to hop into bed myself.

"Why don't you come up to my classroom and write with
the kids?" Gloria asked.

Of course I accepted. She had called my bluff, and I could
never let on to her how terrified I was that the kids might
hate me. I spent hours poring over ideas culled from the
other writers' work, and once a week I would ride the sub-
way to East Harlem and enter the aging archetypal brick

monument/mausoleum that was P.S. Something-or-Other. Gloria's kids and I wrote invisible notes in lemon juice, wrote backwards, and then rushed to the mirror on the door of her coat closet to decipher it. They wrote about having to stay in their apartments when they returned from school to avoid the shootings and stabbings they could chronicle all too well for their tender years.

God knows what Gloria threatened her kids with before my weekly appearances, but she created for me the same safe environment she constructed for her children, where I could explore, look stupid, fall on my face, and return to try again.

CHAPTER 4

Heading for the Real
Our Town

Gloria's classroom was the magic wardrobe through which I eventually walked into my own classroom. Not long after, together with two other Teachers and Writers Collaborative administrators, also eager to trade their office desks for teachers' desks, several staff members and I left the program to set up a writing resource center in a rural Vermont school district.

Since our band of urban waifs came with its own small foundation grant, all we needed from the local superintendent was a chunk of unused space and his blessing on our writing resource center as an approved part of the district's educational program.

Into that charmless cinder block room the size of two ordinary classrooms with a view of the as yet unopened interstate highway, we crammed a crazy-quilt collection of materials—a stage in one corner, a darkroom in another, printing presses, secondhand typewriters scavenged at local auctions, study lofts constructed with the help of our young students more practiced in the building trade than we, even a mysterious shower stall in the center of the room whose purpose was unclear even to us but that we hoped would inspire some fanciful writing.

The students came to us at intervals from their regular classrooms, and many stayed after school, intrigued by this new presence in their community. Terry, whom many considered slow, wrote an elaborate set of instructions for the use of the darkroom. John, a witty, irreverent sixth grader, wrote satirical plays that were performed on our eighteen-inch-high stage. Regina, part of a large Irish clan that constituted a significant proportion of our school population, wrote poems about her horses and printed them on our primitive presses, discards from old print shops.

When a teacher retired unexpectedly, the superintendent encouraged me to take over her classroom. He was able to offer teacher certification under a loophole—now undoubtedly long since closed—that gave superintendents the authority to certify anyone in their district whose presence in the classroom might be of educational benefit to the children.

That invitation came at a time when the resource center's drop-in format was becoming a frustration to us, unintegrated as it was with the work of the regular classrooms. Now we were in a position to make movies as part of our Eskimo unit in social studies, keep journals during our science study of the hatching of a monarch butterfly from its chrysalis.

That classroom of fifth and sixth graders in Fairlee, Vermont, gave me my first taste of control over my own educational turf, and except for an interlude of several years when I was training other fledgling teachers in a graduate teacher education program, I have never been away from a classroom of my own, never missed a summer contemplating the new projects, new readings, new relationships that awaited me in the fall.

Fairlee was no rural idyll. After our second year in the school, we were informed that our contracts would not be renewed. Many parents were delighted with our work and supported us in whatever way their busy lives allowed. Our reputation was drawing teachers from surrounding schools to our workshops, where they could play with the same stimulating materials and ideas our students were using in the writing resource center.

But there were those who were offended by nearly everything we did. Textbooks were nowhere in evidence. Children, no longer anchored to desks, sprawled on the carpet to read and write. The classroom vibrated with the noise generated by their collaborative projects. The in-class bathroom overflowed with plastic jugs, rolls of ribbon, Styrofoam, and other material scavenged for future classroom projects. These outsiders/big city people/Jews (at least some of us) were importing alien ideas and threatening the prevailing way of life, as that life was defined by two of the three school board members.

We were young, self-righteous, convinced of the correctness of our ways and the ignorance and mean-spiritedness of those who opposed them—and we paid the price. The local teacher organization offered to take up our cause, but we recognized that the delicate threads that bound school and community had been frayed beyond repair and it was time to move on, much to the relief of even our supporters, who had begun to pine for the quieter times that predated the rainmakers' arrival in town.

Teachers are so often made to feel powerless by administrators and bureaucratic machinery that constrain them from following their own good judgment or coerce them to perform in ways that clearly run contrary to that judgment. Yet within their classrooms, teachers can experience a novelist's sense of power, the license to create a world of their own design. In rare instances, that power is directed malevolently to satisfy neurotic needs at the expense of children, just as some parents prey on children. But for the most part, teachers aspire to use their godly powers to create the safest, happiest, most productive environments possible for their children. It was that life-affirming hope—illusion though it may prove to be—of creating a new utopia every fall that hooked me on teaching and that drives so many other dedicated teachers I know.

I spent three years in the safe haven of a graduate teacher education program I directed at a branch of Antioch College in southern New Hampshire. There I reflected on the lessons of Fairlee. I visited my interns in buildings that ran from gray cinder block to idyllic nineteenth-century clapboard, from one room to six. They sat on town squares facing the bandstand; in shadeless fields alongside the state highway; around sharp bends in hilly roads.

The appeal of all this was enormous, particularly at a time when so many of us had taken up the "small is beautiful" rallying cry. I helped organize a conference of teachers working in one-, two-, and three-room schoolhouses all over northern New England. By the time I was finished listening to their tales of how they juggled six grades in one room and experimented out of necessity with what educational innovators were calling peer tutoring, I knew that I wanted a small school of my own. So when the job came open in Bennington, I applied. It was to be the first of two extended posts that ultimately deposited me at Jones.

When I arrived in Bennington, a New York Jew with a Ph.D. from Harvard in a *Judenrein* blue-collar rural town where junked cars outnumbered bookcases, there was ample reason to question the match.

I had gone to see the town's representative on the regional school board in the general store he ran in a neighboring town. When there was a respite from cutting slabs of cheddar cheese and ringing up neighborhood kids' nickel and dime purchases, I posed the question: "What about someone like me in a community like yours?"

"As long as everything goes well," he said, "nobody will care that you're a Jew, a big-city guy, an egghead. But if anything goes wrong, all of that will surface."

His assessment was never tested because, in fact, nothing major did go wrong in my six years at Bennington. Perhaps I never risked threatening the townsfolk, but I like to think that I had learned a bit of judiciousness since that first small-town job, where, inflamed by the spirit of the sixties, I approached each decision like an adolescent intent on outraging his bewildered parents. By the time I arrived in Bennington, I had learned to save my energy for the battles that really count.

We tried to remember to run the flag up the flagpole every morning, and on the days when we forgot, someone from the VFW called to remind us. This was a community that took its patriotism seriously. Although Memorial Day was a school holiday, every teacher and almost every student assembled on the school porch to be issued an American flag mounted on a thin dowel, retrieved from basement storage. Somehow, here, close to the source of the original impulse, patriotism felt more like an affirmation, a giving of thanks, than a mean-spirited nose thumbing at a threatening outside world.

I recently came upon a photograph of Bennington's Pierce School taken by one of my students as part of a project in which we photographed all the public places in town and wrote about the memories and experiences students associated with them. The roster of public places wasn't too vast in a town of six hundred: the school, the town hall, the post office, the general store, the fire station, the churches, the paper mill, the VFW hall, the town park and ball field, and the two restaurants that drew on a clientele beyond the boundaries of the town. That was it. Photos of all these places had emerged from the darkroom we installed in the chilly basement of the school, and we all acknowledged that the stark black and white images often looked better than the places themselves, perhaps because they were abstracted from their seedy surroundings. No one would ever see them in such pure, majestic isolation.

The school building in that photo projects solidity and permanence. At the fiftieth-anniversary celebration, we sank a time capsule into the grass beside the flagpole, and none of us doubted that the building would still be there in another fifty years when it was time to unearth the capsule. Two stories tall, the red brick building had a front porch supported by two white Greek Revival columns that ran the full height of the building.

And the interior! Dark wood paneling, chest high in all the classrooms and the hallways. Long wardrobes with black coat hooks that lacked only sliding doors to replicate those of my Brooklyn childhood in which we hid when the teacher was out of the room and that hosted the first fumbling sexual encounters for many a young student. Every classroom had an old-fashioned wind-up pendulum clock mounted above the blackboard. Since there was no full-time administrator, the office wasn't even equipped with a desk, just a kind of dining room table beside the ditto machine and what is described in school budgets as the consumable supplies, a label that conjures up images of paper- and crayon-eating beasts with hairy bodies and enormous teeth. Whenever the phone on the office wall rang, a student monitor in one of the adjacent rooms would answer it and rush to summon whoever was needed. It was via this primitive signal system that I was called forth one day from my basement classroom to receive the news that my mother had died in New York.

For Pierce School as structure, the medium was the message. The solidity of the place declared that it was a significant anchor in the community and planned to continue being just that. The land and the building had been donated to the town by Mr. Arthur Pierce, then the owner of the paper mill. As the major employer, the mill was the community's real anchor, and in the spirit of enlightened self-interest that characterizes the best of American business, Mr. Pierce was sending a message with his gift about the relationship between education and a much-to-be-desired community stability.

In February or March, for example, the town hall was packed for the annual school play. Later, in Houston, such an event would draw only the parents of the performers, but in Bennington, far from the competitive tug of the Galleria, Jones Hall, Wortham Center, and the fourteen-screen Cineplex movie theater, the school play was literally the only show in town.

To do *Tom Sawyer* in such a setting was to experience the epitome of life imitating art: the parts were not exactly a stretch for the cast. When Tom and Huck hid in the graveyard and accidentally witnessed the death of Doc Robinson, it was not hard to transpose the entire scene to the town cemetery, which was the site of the Memorial Day salute. And the Sunday school scenes in which Tom traded colored tickets with the other students who had rightfully earned them by memorizing scripture—these could easily have taken place in the Congregational church that sat kitty-corner from the school across what passed for a town square in Bennington. However, I had the distinct impression that few of our kids were going to Sunday school anymore—maybe the Catholics, but not the others. Their families had moved on to the religion of the CB radios that sat in their houses like icons from which they literally awaited the squawking evil decree—who by fire and who by pickup and who by heart attack.

The year ended at the town ball field, site of the annual school picnic. While the kids organized softball games and flew paper airplanes around the Little League field on which Bennington jousted with teams from the neighboring towns, parents and grandparents and teachers were grilling the hamburgers and hot dogs and cutting up the watermelon and pouring the drinks.

The grand finale was a little modern-day embellishment that doesn't quite mesh with the rest of the Norman Rockwell scene. For two weeks before the picnic, the older kids fashioned their own rockets—paper-towel bodies, balsa-wood noses and fins, and garbage-bag parachutes. These painted and often cockeyed contraptions were fitted with hobby shop rocket engines and dispatched from a hill above the ball field with the aid of a car battery. After the countdown and the squeals, some of the rockets streaked majestically to their zeniths, where their garbage-bag parachutes inflated and carried them back to an unpredictable resting place, often a treetop or a neighboring roof. Others, the cockeyed ones, did a crazy zigzag dance thirty or forty feet in the air and plummeted straight back toward second base trailing smoke and sulfurous stink. With that, school was out and David, the local restaurateur, could get that table ready for the teachers' lunch the next day.

The graduating class at Pierce School in Bennington fluctuated between eight and eighteen in my six years there, a far cry from my Brooklyn high school graduating class of twelve hundred.

The graduates sat in metal folding chairs on the stage of

the town hall, the same stage on which we performed *Tom Sawyer* and a version of *Peter Pan*; where the instrument students gave their fall and spring recitals; where the finalists in our annual speaking contest stood to declaim Robert Louis Stevenson and T. S. Eliot and Shel Silverstein before judges in an event whose echo of nineteenth-century *Little House on the Prairie* America never failed to bring sentimental tears to my eyes. In that same hall, the whole school had gathered to see a local farmer demonstrate sheep shearing as part of a unit on wool. The kids rooted for the sheep to crap in the foul circle painted on the town hall floor; a goat had obliged in the middle of a play performance they attended in a neighboring town.

That hall echoed with the ghosts of sweaty after-school basketball scrimmages with kids still a couple of years away from learning that passing was as much a part of the game as shooting. Dance troupes, puppet shows, contra-dance callers, a special extravaganza in honor of the school's fiftieth anniversary. There had been an angry public hearing about another town's plans to dump its garbage in our militantly unzoned town of Bennington. ("Ain't nobody gonna tell us where we can build our houses and where we can put our furniture refinishing business.") At that hearing, a group of students had made a presentation of their research, complete with photographs, showing the proximity of the dump site to the river into which the dump runoff would inevitably leak; the dump never came.

Finally, the moment before the students got their diplomas and assorted honors and certificates came. Each one stood and read a set of memories of his or her years at Pierce School that we had written together during the past few weeks in between collecting the textbooks and scrubbing down the desks and tables. These memories had an intentional religious incantatory quality. Each line began "I remember . . ."

53

and proceeded to recount the time Ronnie farted during the achievement tests, or the time Beth ate a gross doughnut filled with black bean stuff on a school trip to Chinatown in Boston, or the time the boys hid in the girls' bathroom at environmental camp in Maine. It didn't take a trained social psychologist to notice that no one ever included on the list memories that had to do with teaching or learning or books. That's not what kids retain from their years in school, at least not overtly. The collective unconscious of a school consists of fragments of events that break the daily routine of tests and texts and talk—trips, dances, games, gaffes, accidents, injuries, and high jinx.

Is all that not the essence of small-town America, something straight out of Garrison Keillor? Doesn't it tweak the heartstrings of people who grew up in the anomie of the big city or in the blandness of the suburban wasteland? Everything I've described is true, but it's only one side of Bennington. You need to know that if the school worked, it did so in spite of the fact that Bennington was a community with more than its share of social disorganization and human weakness.

More than a decade ago, Michael Lesy, in his book *Wisconsin Death Trip*, scoured nineteenth-century newspapers to reconstruct a rural world of suicide, madness, murder, and arson that had little to do with the uplifting episodes of human nobility on the television version of *Little House on the Prairie* that brought weekly tears to my wife's eyes.

Drinking is the social disease of our time. Places like Bennington and the surrounding towns had all the makings of a distiller's paradise. The winters are long and lonely; people live isolated from each other with few diversions other than their television sets (minus the VCRs at that stage); the prevailing macho culture elevates drink to a central role in all the bonding rituals—at the fire station, at the

VFW hall, and around the chain saws and snowmobiles in the woods. Undoubtedly, though I was less familiar with them, the women were finding their own occasions and locations for drinking as well. As a result, there wasn't a night of the week devoid of an Alcoholics Anonymous meeting in one local town or another.

In this world awash in alcohol vapors, Andy's father drove an oil delivery truck until he was arrested for driving under the influence, then lost his license and his job. From then on, he sat home, drinking, watching television, and making the lives of Andy and his mother miserable. One infamous day Andy waited in the below-zero weather for a school bus that never arrived. When he went back up the driveway to report his dilemma, his father, already well along in his morning consumption, told him to turn his tail around and walk to school. Before the day was over, Andy had heaved a rock through his own front window, flung a chair at a classmate even before he had undone his snowmobile boots, and suffered through a brutal thrashing by his father. Violence or the threat of violence was a daily fact of Andy's life, and it's no surprise that he was dishing out the same at his end of the biological chain.

Always, alcohol lurked behind the torn stage curtain, waiting to disrupt the town's pastoral play being enacted center stage.

And the same was true of sex. Donna was pregnant at fourteen, less than two years out of my class. By the time I left Bennington, her child was approaching school age, ready for the next turn of the wheel. Tammy's sisters had all gotten pregnant in high school, and everyone in town automatically assumed she would follow suit. This sexual equivalent of guilt by association made Tammy's school life miserable because her classmates read into her every move evidence of present or future promiscuity.

As an outsider to the community, I was fortunate enough to have teachers who were of the place untangle for me the complex web of interrelationships, much like an anthropologist's informants in some exotic tribe. In this way I was saved from countless social gaffes and had clarified for me many puzzling relationships among the kids in the school. There were several sets of half siblings, the results of premarital pregnancies followed by later marriages to other partners, the intricacies of which were not always clear to the children themselves. Each of these odd couplings looked to an outsider like a potential time bomb poised to blow the community apart, although things drifted along rather uneventfully.

Most of the other social ills were represented in Bennington, including wife beating, child abuse, and petty crime. All these sordid aspects of what was festering beneath the surface of one small town's life could have provided ample rationalization for why the school wasn't working, couldn't possibly work, was doomed to failure until the great social revolution made the social fabric whole. It's the kind of analysis of inner-city ghetto schools you can read about in the papers every day: politicians, teachers, administrators, even parents throw up their hands and say what can the school do? They don't have stable families, they get pregnant, they do drugs. (Yes, we had parents like those, too, in Bennington.)

But the fact of the matter is that the school in Bennington *did* work.

In a small community school, much of what happens in the classroom could have been lifted from the latest manual of best practices: multiage classrooms, children of varying ability levels sharing the same learning space, small-group work, learning activities growing out of extended projects that integrate a variety of curriculum areas, making use of community resources in the child's education.

All of these seem to flow naturally from the position the school occupies in the community, the inextricable bonds among the community members and the community institutions. The students would be more hard pressed to remember the dailiness of our time together, but I remember the slide show we produced about the work of the town paper mill; the short stories we dramatized for taping; the buzz of children exploring the mysteries of batteries and bulbs in one corner of the room while their classmates stitched books they were binding for publication; the hushed intensity of individual silent reading while in the adjacent room a small team cooked the hot dogs we sold at lunch to finance our next trip to Boston.

These elements of the best of progressive education co-existed with elements that would have been recognizable to these children's' nineteenth-century forebears: committing long poems to memory, reeling off state capitals and names of presidents, progressing through the pages of the math workbook, preparing for the weekly spelling test. It made for a healthy mix of tradition and innovation, well suited for the setting. My big-city colleagues would be surprised to discover the extent to which they have been outdistanced pedagogically by their country cousins.

Any visitor could determine that Pierce School was relatively calm and orderly. Kids felt safe there and could concentrate on their work without fear or extreme threats of punishment. The teachers and staff showed love, concern, and respect for the children. *And* the children were, in fact, learning. In Bennington, there were no illiterates. Everyone learned to read and write. Everyone passed the basic skills test the district required, although that's hardly a criterion I would want to pin our national aspirations on. And there was some room for kids more able in certain areas to reach a bit beyond what their classmates were tackling. It's not the kind of education that gets written up in the education journals, but it's respectable and socially useful.

In Bennington, the school was both the means and the motive for community cohesiveness. The school is often the only entity that provides a small town with a sense of identity. In the frugal New England culture, the citizens of Bennington and the neighboring towns have consistently voted against their pocketbooks by rejecting proposals for school consolidation, which purport to be money savers. People sense that with the disappearance of their town schools comes a hollowness, a lack of social purpose for the community that makes it no more than a grid of streets along which houses are arrayed.

There is a fair bit of transience in a town like Bennington as people slip in and out of the rental properties that continue to be more affordable for young and mobile people than the upscale property in more gentrified towns. Yet there is a stable nucleus of families whose children will go to school together and will continue to form the spine of the community for the rest of their lives. These people have got to see to it that the school works because it is the hatchery for future alliances and relationships. Since Bennington is where you're likely to be bedding down, it would not do to foul your own nest. Consider the fact that in most Chicago schools at least one-third of the students who begin school in September will have moved on by June.

The majority of people in Bennington are not going anywhere, partly for lack of choice or vision, but also because it's not a bad place to live. There are enough ways to get by economically; there's an abundance of pretty, open land for getting wood, riding snowmobiles, or just plain admiring;

and there's a frontier sense of being able to live your life without an undue number of restrictions and constraints. In the midst of a great deal that doesn't work well in the personal lives of its inhabitants, it is doubly important that these citizens contract to make their school a much-needed social adhesive.

Small towns and urban neighborhoods are tethered to the schools that serve them like climbers negotiating a steep ascent. Neither advances without the help of the other, but if one stumbles, it's a long way to the bottom for both.

CHAPTER **5**

From Our Town
to Big Town

When I left New York in 1971 with my wife and two small
daughters, I thought I had said good-bye to the city forever.
For eleven years we lived a life of gardening, maple sugar-
ing, town meetings, community choruses, and small-town
newspapers that reported towel thefts from the local motel
in their police logs. I stopped smoking, began jogging,
learned to cross-country ski, to split wood, and to use hand-
saws, chain saws, jigsaws, and circular saws—I who had
eschewed contact with all tools after my disastrous forced
labor in the shop classes of my technical high school in
Brooklyn.

They were wonderful years. My children grew up in the
safe world of their small-town schools, whose buses picked
them up and deposited them efficiently in front of our red
mailbox, deterred only by the occasional snowstorm. They—
all of us, in fact—were insider/outsiders, a term coined by
an old German/Jewish émigré friend wise in the subtleties of
marginality. We were willingly enmeshed in the life of our
adopted community but maintained a psychic apartness
patented by generations of Jewish forebears.

After six solid years as teacher and principal in my small New Hampshire elementary school, I was ready to try something different, so I did what wives often do—follow the spouse with the assured job and see what happens. My wife had been offered a job teaching writing in Houston, and after first dismissing the idea of leaving Nirvana for freeways and crime, we decided we were up for a new adventure. I thought I might write or get involved in child advocacy work. I didn't know exactly what, but I was sure the Mr. Right of jobs would declare itself when I opened myself to new possibilities.

I lasted for exactly three weeks in my freelance life before a student in my wife's writing class suggested that I check on an unusual middle school that her daughter attended. She had heard they were short an English teacher.

The drive out to T. H. Rogers School was an experience in culture shock, not just in relation to New Hampshire, but even over and against the near-downtown neighborhood where we were living. Our part of town was the old, pre-boom Houston of tree-lined streets and houses aging with a character that an unsympathetic eye might perceive as seediness. In many big cities, the modern-day equivalent of the walls that girdled the old town and protected it from marauders is the Loop, a ring highway that is the demarcation line between the artsy, decadent, dangerous heart of the city and its scrubbed Formica outlands that people presume to be more hospitable to family life and its accoutrements.

Rogers was definitely outside the Loop, set amid townhouse complexes and glass office towers still harsh in their newness. The landscaping and the pencil-thin trees had not yet taken hold in the uninviting Houston combination of gumbo soil and withering sun. Only a few blocks east, on the Loop's edge, lay the Galleria, the granddaddy of American shopping meccas, a bracelet of indoor high-style shops and department stores ringing an ice-skating rink where one could forget the ninety-degree-plus temperatures and the 80-percent-plus-or-minus humidity lying in ambush outside the electric-eye doors.

Rogers itself was a confused hybrid of old and new. Once it had been a neighborhood junior high school, closed, some say, because of declining school population in the area, and others say as a punitive retaliation against the efforts by residents in the area to secede from the Houston Independent School District to form their own minority-rein zone. Once free of its neighborhood obligations, the school underwent major renovation and retouching to prepare it to house two seemingly mismatched nonzoned programs, one for multiply handicapped and deaf students, and one for gifted students who would eventually span the grades from kindergarten to eighth. The recently acquired series of symmetrical humps visible along one side of its perimeter turned out to be the special bathroom and changing facilities needed for each classroom of handicapped students.

I don't know whether the wedding of these programs that seemed to have so little in common was an act of administrative vision and genius or a result of bureaucratic expediency, but the Rogers staff—and I among them when I eventually signed on—spent a good deal of energy trying to make a programmatic virtue of the cards we had been dealt. Gifted students studied sign language, went off with deaf students for retreats and outdoor adventure experiences, and volunteered as aides in classrooms of severely handicapped students. At every step, the best and the brightest were surrounded by the humbling evidence of the thin line they all walked between privilege and incapacity. The human spirit that inhabited such broken, damaged bodies was there to remind our gifted students, who already wore their elite college futures like airline luggage tags, that intellect and the verbal facility to display it are not the sole definers of humanity.

But I am getting far ahead of my story. On that very first day in the sterile semisuburbs of Houston, I sat in the holding pen of Rogers's main office waiting for an interview with the principal, watching the parade of wheelchairs, bright-faced monitors (school had already been in session for three weeks by this time), and a colorfully diverse staff: a bearded young man wearing a yarmulke, a striking black woman wrapped in her own distinctive head covering—a striped bandana—and two eager young teachers busily signing and grunting as they passed, oblivious to their fascinated audience. It occurred to me that this was a world I could easily inhabit. I was hungry to be readmitted to the maddening universe of the educational wage slave, where, in return for vows of poverty, you were permitted entrée into the precious and comical lives of children and their keepers, an endless source of entertainment and reward for those with a novelistic temperament.

The principal who summoned me to her office was a lusty maverick of a woman, unselfconsciously overweight and owner of a broad Texas accent that seemed as much of a media stereotype as my New York accent must have been to her. As I learned over the next four years, she laughed hard, was fiercely loyal to her staff, and possessed a genius for wringing from the central office the resources and the license to run her quirky school, which just refused to fit comfortably inside the straitjacket guidelines that prevail in the rest of the system. How anyone like her could have survived the Byzantine yes-man educational bureaucracy and risen to the position of principal was a political wonder.

Her departure was as dramatic as her tenure. At the closing day staff luncheon at the end of my fourth year, she seized the portable mike from a previous speaker, flipped on some farewell music she had recorded to play on her boom box, and announced to her stunned staff that she was moving on to California. I imagine her spirit had had its fill of small-minded constraint, and she was striking out for a place where she fancied her free spirit might find a more congenial home, where it would not be used as a bludgeon by one of the vindictive administrators she had outfoxed.

But on that first day, with my résumé in hand, she questioned me across her desk in terms that made it clear that she needed me as much as I needed her. She called me doctor every chance she got, already savoring the coup she could present to the frantically ambitious parents of her gifted students. A Harvard Ph.D. to teach their children!

When I left Bennington, the third graders presented me with a T-shirt on which each of the children had inscribed his or her name in fabric paint. Their artistic teacher had lettered a decorative MR. H across the chest. Those kids would be amused at hearing me called "Dr. Hoffman" in Houston. Except for my college teaching years at Tougaloo, I had never been called doctor. On the contrary! In my early public school days, I toyed with having kids call me by my first name, but I backed off. Titles carry symbolic weight: authority, control, respect. Parents would misunderstand, and I had battles to fight on too many other fronts.

I don't take well to people trafficking in assigned and ascribed authority, qualities that need to be earned. Yet I never raised a fuss here about being called doctor. In any case, titles go down more easily in the South, with its aristocratic history, than they do in egalitarian New England.

What a fascinatingly rich and diverse lot these families were. Rogers had drawn them from great distances across this sprawling city in their search for a school that would challenge their children and save them from the cookie-cutter neighborhood schools that often failed to recognize that boredom and occasional misbehavior spring from a need to be challenged and extended. The absence of any cohesive physical community bound by common history, by interlocking family ties, by shared community institutions was a world apart from my earlier experience in New Hampshire. In spite of the inevitable small-town rifts and vendettas, the school there worked well because it was built on a shared set of values—hard work, rugged independence, and patriotism. In more sophisticated circles, many of these values and their manner of expression appear either quaint or passé, but in the small town they worked well for people who intended to remain rooted in their communities.

At Rogers, the binding values revolved around the individual, not the community. There was a shared belief that achievement and academic success open all doors to society's treasure house. Unlike the rooted population of rural New Hampshire, many of the Rogers parents were immigrants or the children of immigrants—Indians, Asians, Israelis, Eastern Europeans, Central Americans, transplanted rural Southern blacks and whites, small-town Anglos come to the big city to make good. They were hungry for a piece of the American Dream, and the school was to be the vehicle for hacking off their slice. Mr. Tran, rumored to have been a colonel in the Vietnamese army, appeared at my classroom door weekly to ask how his son David was progressing and whether anything could be done to improve the quality of his English (which was already impeccable). Mrs. K, a recent arrival from Russia, wanted to be certain that her son Michael was getting the proper math background to qualify him for Ivy League admission. Paradoxically, their highly individualistic goals bound them together to support the school through their political assaults on the bureaucracy downtown and through their volunteer and fund-raising efforts. They recognized the need to forge a temporary community that could

be dismantled when it had achieved its goal, like a base camp
thrown up for an assault on a mountain peak.

One of the remarkable by-products of the shared purpose
that defined this community was the surprising degree of social harmony among the students, in spite of the turbulence
that marked so much of the society that surrounded it. In my
six years at Rogers, I cannot remember a moment of ugliness
among our black, white, Asian, and Hispanic population.
Whatever the unvoiced animosities, they remained subordinated to the shared purpose of moving everyone along the
path to economic and academic success. Only at the entry
and exit points was this harmony breached to any degree.
Here, differential admission standards to Rogers and, later,
to selected high schools, came into play, placing members of
the community in uncharacteristically competitive positions
with one another. The toxins of affirmative action temporarily poisoned parts of the entire community at these points,
but not enough to wreak any permanent damage on the
community's otherwise healthy body.

There was a second group of parents and kids who desperately needed the school and were determined to make it
work. These were the misfits, kids unsuited for what passed
for the normal teenage world. For them, the goal was not so
much achievement as sheer survival, negotiating the treach-
erous straits of early adolescence en route to a less judgmen-
tal, more tolerant adulthood.

Lauren was the kind of kid her peers branded without
hesitation as weird. She rarely made eye contact when she
addressed you. Her face was deeply pitted with acne, her
hair unkempt and unwashed. When she spoke, it was in
unmodulated tones. Words erupted from her in an almost
bellicose way, and her utter lack of social skills invariably
alienated her audience. Many days in class she buried herself in a book by resting her head on her arms and dropped

off to a very public sleep. In another school, Lauren would have been dead meat. But here, everyone was a misfit of sorts. At a school dance, a seventh grader once said to me, "Look at all those people out there dancing. In any other school, we'd be wallflowers." Though not entirely free of adolescent cruelty, the students were more compassionate than most. The girls invited Lauren to shop with them, gave her tips about washing her hair. They did not rise to the bait of her aggressive verbal assaults. In short, they went more than halfway to accept her in all her strangeness, and though they were not hugely rewarded for it, they made school a far more tolerable place for Lauren.

Colorful misfits abounded—and were tolerated among the teaching staff as well. Mr. V, a flamboyantly gay art teacher, came dressed one Halloween as a cloud, his long, bleached blond hair standing out against the billowy puffs he had affixed to his shoulders like angel wings. For years he had sponsored the cheerleaders, coaching them with mincing steps through their assorted routines, until one day he was gone, reassigned to the central office for special duty. A year later he was dead, the first victim of AIDS I knew personally, a harbinger of a less innocent era to come.

The flamboyant woman with the colorful headband who passed me that first day outside the principal's office was a rare find. Charlotte was a teacher of severely retarded and handicapped young children. She was in her mid-fifties, strikingly handsome and well-preserved enough to have married a man almost the age of her talented Broadway musical star son from a previous marriage. Charlotte was a fellow Brooklynite, and I delighted in hearing an accent identical to mine emerge unexpectedly form that black visage. Even now, years since my departure from Rogers, she calls on my birthday, and I assume she provides the same service

for every other present and former Rogers staff person inscribed in her register.

Mrs. Miller, aka the Raccoon Lady, had been working
with handicapped students for more than twenty-five years.
In her dungarees and work shirt, she looked tough and
ready for business. By all testimony, she was competent in
her classroom, but her heart was really back home with her
raccoons. She had been designated by the Wildlife Service as
a handler of raccoons. Animals injured by cars or separated
early from their mothers were brought to her for rehabilita-
tion. When she was done ministering to them, she released
them in a distant wooded area—all except one wily creature
who had been with her for years and who had become such
a central player in her life that she decided to write a book
about him. Since I was "the writing teacher," it fell to me to
read these charming but clumsily written tales of the practi-
cal jokes Sparky played on her: stealing her car keys, hiding
in the bathroom hamper. I invited her into my English class
to talk about Sparky and justified it as a stimulus to reading
the many animal stories with which I had stocked the class
library. The days that stand out for the students amid the sea
of faceless others are often those in which the teacher allows
a bit of her or his life "outside" to intrude into the classroom;
they can sense real passion and value it above the manufac-
tured variety. Mrs. Miller and her raccoons were the real
thing, as was a political cartoonist for one of the Houston
papers who had two daughters in the school and was always
willing to come by to talk and draw with the kids, a much-
needed breath of the real world in the locker-lined, eerily
silent halls of T. H. Rogers.

Somehow the glue held and the odd and intriguing collection of students, teachers, and parents built a stable little
world that was exciting to enter every morning, a world in

which typical discipline problems involved running in the hall, although we had our share—and more—of fire setters, attempted suicides, devil worshippers, experimental drinkers, and weapons carriers during my six years there. Yet for a teacher raised on egalitarian principles, every day in that school was an immersion in guilt and ambivalence. Was it right to be skimming these wonderful children, the cream of their neighborhood schools, from their less academically gifted peers? What were the losses for each of the groups? Were our successes at Rogers coming at the expense of neighborhood schools, which were being drained as surely as a rural community whose most energetic and enterprising citizens migrate to the big city?

The pleasures of engaging such bright minds, up to any challenge, left unanswered the question of whether it was right to cluster these kids in the same room. In the midst of good sex, does one fade to a split-screen vision of the forlorn at home alone, grimly laying out their clothes for another drab workday?

Let me give you a little glimpse of how much fun a place like Rogers can be for teachers and kids alike. It is my sixth and final year at the school. Nostalgic for the school productions I directed in the little town hall in Bennington, New Hampshire, I have managed to include in my schedule just this once an elective in dramatics. Although I am devoid of stage talent, I am like the minor league utility infielder elevated to major league manager. I know all the right moves without being able to execute them myself. I was once seduced into taking the only adult role in a children's summer theater. As a mad scientist, Dr. Cacophonous A. Discord, in *The Phantom Tollbooth*, I was the only cast member who had difficulty learning his lines. At best, I was tolerated by my fellow cast members.

Now here I was with twelve enthusiastic eighth graders

seated in a circle on the carpeted floor of my classroom. Every day, this extraordinary crew of Israelis, Russian émigrés, blacks, Hispanics, and Anglos careened through dramatic exercises, improvisations, role-playing scenarios, dramatic readings, and original one-act plays. We spent our last month together preparing a production of a wickedly funny send-up of small-town Texas life called *Greater Tuna*. In the original version the play's eighteen or so characters were performed by two actors, but by surgically separating the roles I was able to accommodate the entire class. Two weeks before I left Rogers for good we performed *Greater Tuna* for the entire school community. The kids transformed themselves into radio announcers, small-town eccentrics, ministers, rifle enthusiasts—the whole colorful panoply of human dignity and foolishness that constitutes small-town life in America.

As I watched this parade of fools and saints from my favorite position alongside the spotlight operator in the upper tier of the school's multipurpose performance room, I marvelled at the fact that here in Houston, the very antithesis of the small town, we had re-created, from disparate pieces, within this cold, functional building, our own community of purpose. Each school is a community. Some serve their members well and some could fashionably be called dysfunctional. This crazy-quilt cosmos of gifted, deaf, and handicapped kids that was T. H. Rogers constituted a community without benefit of volunteer fire department or defining church. It was a voluntary association like the medieval tower societies whose members were drawn together in recognition of the mutual protective benefits to be derived from their association. All families and all children should be linked to their own tower society in which they can seek shelter and common purpose. The alternative is a few isolated, heavily fortified defense bastions, surrounded by angry, excluded hordes. That prospect is too awful to contemplate.

On the last day of school, teachers really let their hair down. I'm talking about that extra day tacked on to the calendar after the kids are gone. Yesterday we stood on the hot loading ramp waving to the departing buses. Therman, the coolest of dudes, was slumped in the back seat he owned as a graduating eighth grader, his eyes full of tears. Some of the younger kids were hanging out the windows waving back at us. They knew they would be back next year. No reason for tears, unless it was for the summer of numbing boredom that stretched beyond the first few days of nonstop sleeping and watching TV. Some of them would soon be looking back nostalgically on these last few days of pizza parties, leisurely treks to the book room with stacks of science textbooks, video viewing, talent shows—the stock-in-trade of the end of the year pacification program.

That was yesterday. Today there are empty lockers, their doors standing open like a giant domino pattern, awaiting a starter to topple them. The teachers have shown up in jeans, sandals, T-shirts, shorts, to pack up the last boxes, take down the last photosynthesis posters, load the final plants from the window ledges into their cars, tape wrapping paper over the last bookcase in a ritual that has become detached over the years from its original dust-prevention purpose. All that remains is to dart through the corridors collecting initials on the long checklist ("Return firetags to Mrs. Gordon"; "Submit list of unreturned textbooks to Mrs. Knox"), which, when it is completed, will liberate that last paycheck.

This final student-free day ends with the staff sitting down to eat together. No religious ritual is complete without the breaking of bread. In my little New Hampshire school, our enormous workforce of four would close out the year by crossing the tiny town square to eat lunch at David's, a little restaurant more in step with Soho than with this steak and potatoes blue-collar town. In Houston, the sheer scale of things dictated a different modus operandi. We were a staff of 150, not easily fed in a neighborhood restaurant, so every year the parents hosted an appreciation lunch in the school cafeteria. Teachers, aides, and administrators dutifully lined up in the cafetorium to file past the serving trays of fried chicken, coleslaw, and potato salad, the Styrofoam kegs of iced tea, and the dishes of homemade desserts. The cafetorium is a dual-purpose space intended for use as both a cafeteria and an auditorium, and suitable for neither. I finally gave up on trying to produce my plays in that space when I realized that only Liza Minnelli could ever succeed in making herself heard beyond the third row.

At this end-of-year lunch, the parents appeared to be playing the very traditional roles of food preparers and servers, throwbacks to the days of nonworking women with the time to be professional volunteers.

Like every good corporate entity, the Houston Independent School District gives out service pins—five years, ten years, all the way up to thirty! Then those who won't be back next year are called on to say good-bye and explain where their lives are taking them. Since I was leaving after six years for a different job in the district, I lined up at the microphone right behind the home ec teacher, who upstaged me by announcing that she had been told minutes before that there was no job for her at the school next year.

When I finally took my place at the mike, I was aware that the parent servers had moved down to the front of the cafetorium from their position at the serving table and were lined up behind me, a friendly firing squad. After I was done, they held out to me a telephone-book-sized leatherbound volume with gold letters on the spine announcing

Musings, 1983–1988: five years worth of issues of the school
literary magazine, which I had kept afloat over the years
on a sea of hastily eaten lunches. This was the kind of book
nobody actually owned. You called it forth from the bowels
of the library when you needed a quote from the *Journal of
Political Geography* for your term paper.

This formidable presence on my humid Houston book-
shelf has acquired a patina of mildew in the years since. I
flip through it from time to time to revisit the extraordinary
cast of middle schoolers who were my life for six years.
Nothing—not Shakespeare, Dostoyevsky, Dickens—was beyond their reach. One could only weep for the vast majority
of students elsewhere of whom nothing was expected and
who performed accordingly.

Nonetheless, it was time to move on again. My youngest
daughter was about to graduate from high school. My pattern of moving up through the grades with my children was
lagging. It was time to get on to high school, where I could
test myself in the presence of older students, where I would
have access to both the talented Vanguard students and the
"regular" kids, and where I would be able to use my classroom as a demonstration site, part of a teacher-development
project in writing sponsored by Rice University.

One final farewell to my classroom, now stripped down
to bare-wall simplicity, ready for habitation by next year's
teacher, who will undoubtedly attack the bulletin board with
more vigor than I. Soon I will be driving through the west
end of town for the last time, past the doll house-like town
home developments, past the wide avenues lined with restaurants and clubs that will overflow with swinging young
lawyers and management trainees come Friday night.

Like a career foreign service officer or military man, I
was off to a new posting, excited by the prospect of change,

scared that my good luck might finally have run out. Would I now be exposed as the fraudulent self that I suspect many of us secretly conceal behind our confident facades? Almost fifty, I had to begin to ask how many more postings there would be.

PART THREE

Behind the Scenes at Jones

CHAPTER 6

Getting Ready

Twice a week the garbage trucks wheeze their way through our Houston neighborhood. From up the street you can hear the air brakes, followed by an undifferentiated chatter, then the animal rumbling of the compactor as the trash disappears into the belly of the truck. When the whole operation finally comes into view, two men (shirtless if the season is right) sprint along behind the truck, heaving trash bags into the rear-mounted jaws. The truck stops as infrequently as possible, and the men rarely break stride. From time to time you can hear a shout or a whistle, some primitive signal system that passes between the driver and the heavers, somehow controlling the flow of this fast-paced ballet.

Whenever I am home from school on a garbage pickup day, I watch this scene with great fascination. I love to observe people going about their work. The A&P fruit section manager whistles as he stacks and arranges the heads of broccoli. Where is there room for the unique flair that adds an individual touch to the work? How much of the work style is prescribed by those who pass the work culture on to the trainees who follow them? What are the secrets of the trade hidden from the sight of the general public? What really goes on in the restaurant kitchen or in the back store-rooms of the supermarket? How does the manager determine how many cases of lettuce to order? In the case of the garbage men, I want to know why they're hustling all the time. Is there incentive pay for collecting more, for finishing faster? Are they aiming to get off earlier?

For decades now the *Paris Review* has been publishing "Writers at Work," a series of interviews with famous writers about their work styles. Because the subjects of these interviews are cultural icons, we are fascinated by how often they sharpen their pencils, whether they use a word processor, how many hours a day they work, and whether their desk faces a window or a blank wall. I've conducted interviews very similar to these with scientists, another of our priestly classes. I understand little of the substance of their highly technical world, but I wanted to know all I could about how they went about it. How did they spend their time? How did they make key decisions about directions to pursue? To whom did they talk about the choices?

Very few people ask these questions of garbagemen or garage mechanics. One of the people I respect most in the world is my mechanic. I have spent many hours in the bay of his seedy gas station peering over his shoulder as he's poked and prodded under the hood of my car. When I can muster the courage to ask him to think aloud for me, what emerges is a brilliant stream of diagnostic musings that I will match, deduction for deduction, against those of any ten high-earning internists.

And he never lets go of a problem. Once my car contracted a particularly impenetrable ailment that prevented it from holding its idle when my foot was off the gas. For several nights in a row, Bill was still up treating my patient at eleven o'clock. I could see him in there when I drove by. The lights

were on behind the closed bay doors and Bill was staring my
Omni down, trying to hypnotize it into yielding up its secret
to him, which it finally did. I have tried that staring ploy and
I've pulled at the distributor wires and fussed with the hoses
in Bill's authoritative style, but it doesn't seem to produce the
same results for me. I'll just have to content myself with the
pleasure I take in watching him at his sacred work.

The work of teachers arouses as little curiosity from the
general public as that of garbagemen and mechanics. Perhaps
the fact that all of us have spent at least twelve years in the
thrall of one teacher or another is sufficient to convince us
that we already know all we ever care to know about teaching. Just as children growing up together in a kibbutz youth
house are unlikely ever to fall in love with one another, our
close proximity to teachers over the years has demystified
teaching to the point of disrespect. Everybody automatically
assumes that of course they know how teaching is done, and
in fact that they could do it better than the practitioners
they've seen.

Much work, done well, shares a unique quality of ap-
pearing effortless. I've savored such magical moments myself, when I have sat back and watched this benevolent
dybbuk inhabit the body of my classroom and carry it along
unbidden and uninstructed by me. A project takes shape
or a presentation is made that has a life of its own and you
wonder why anyone is paying you to be a teacher.

I often have the same reaction when I see a good administrator at work. What's the big deal? A bit of tact, some respect for the people working under and alongside you, and a
modicum of organization. It's only when you see someone
fail at it, create dissension and chaos, that you begin to realize how many subtle decisions and choices, how much clever
strategy, consciously and unconsciously applied, lie behind
successful practice.

Let me adopt the stance of Bill, my mechanic, as I think aloud about my teaching plans, just as he would conspire to get my Omni up and running again.

It is about a month from the day that school opens. I stare unseeing out the window behind my desk. There is a huge array of decisions to be made between now and then. If I choose well they will become invisible, like the supporting struts inside the finished wall of a sturdy house. I have been ruminating over these issues for months now, ever since I decided that I would be changing jobs and schools for the first time in six years, moving to Jones High School. So many previously resolved issues are reopened as a result of the change. In my old room, I moved the furniture around for four years before I found a configuration of tables that conveyed the message I wanted these students to hear—that they could work together in small groups and that their primary focus was each other, not me. The setup didn't always produce the desired result, but the potential was there. The center of the room contained a large, open carpeted space. When I felt the need to be really informal, we abandoned our chairs and hunkered down in a big circle right in that space. Then the conditions were right to gripe or feel close, an occasion for all of us literally to be on the same level.

Above the banks of bookshelves ran a window shelf bursting with plants, one of them almost six feet high, partner with the Mexican blankets in slicing through the institutional chill. Amid the tangle of green stood a wooden bust, presumably of me, carved by a student and inscribed "To the Best Bald Teacher." Message: It's okay to be irreverent, to joke with me within limits. I might even break out into a baldness soliloquy on the order of the nose speech delivered by Steve Martin, whose modern-day Cyrano can reel off twenty devastating insults to his own beak in *Roxanne.*

I visit my new classroom at Jones. Like a househunter,

you have to try to see beyond what exists to what might be wrought with a few well-conceived transformations. The trash baskets are overflowing with the previous inhabitant's castoffs. Five formidable file cabinets dominate one wall of the room; my predecessor was department chair, a record keeper and documenter. The room is filled with classic exam chairs. Is there an official name for those cursed objects with the fixed arm on which to rest your test paper or your binder? Strapped into this contraption, every man is alone, pitting his triumphs against those of his adversaries, never to reach out and join forces with them. That stuff had to go.

I stop by the principal's office to request that the file cabinets be dispersed among the other needy rooms, the chairs replaced with tables, and the double-locked closet pried open and liberated for communal purposes. In the slack summer calm that descends upon school offices, the principal is more approachable than he will be in the late-August frenzy of school opening. I have made my first crucial pedagogical decisions for the year. I still have to figure out how to arrange the space; again, what will look like a casually arrived at arrangement will be as fussed over and as calculating as the living room prepared with great care for the seduction scene. Where does the teacher's desk go, and what does that tell us about the guy who operates in this space? Does he hold court from behind or does he just use it as a place to unload his papers? That's important.

I used to be far more preoccupied with space arrangement and the physical environment of my classroom than I am today. I was working with younger children then, and the surroundings in which they work are particularly crucial. In those years I spent weeks building special furniture, hunting down used typewriters, cajoling my wife into sewing curtains for the classroom windows. (Although my father was a tailor and spent his life in front of a sewing machine, he did not pass this skill to me. In my family, we have regressed to the sexist impasse that relegates sewing to the womenfolk.) Anyone who's been in middle school or high school lately has surely noticed that attention to aesthetics is on a level comparable to that of your favorite auto-body shop. Better surroundings would undoubtedly enhance learning for these older students as well, but they don't inhabit the same space all day; at least they get to change nondescript locations every hour or so. The simple fact is that I just don't have the time and energy to invest in the physical details any longer. Like everything else, it becomes a matter of priorities, and I have decided on priorities that are less tangible but of greater interest to me at this stage.

Selecting the year's reading is one of those priorities and is very much on my mind at this point in the summer. It's a time I look forward to, a chance to scan the shelves of my library at home, browse in my local bookstore, leaf through old reading lists, and brainstorm with friends and family about what I want to lay before my kids this year. As my list of possibilities proliferates, I get excited over the prospect of introducing some of the books I love to an audience inno- cent of them. The seeds of my discontent are there as well. I know that I will have to drop most of the books on the list for lack of time and hope to get to them another year. Each deletion is like abandoning a loved child.

When the final cut comes, the process will be akin to creating a balanced party ticket for the fall elections. I need to look for minority representation, a balance of male and female protagonists, nonfiction as well as fiction, classic ver- sus contemporary reading, plays as well as novels, comedy alongside more somber material, young adult versus adult books, books with easily accessible language and structure and those that will be a stretch for the students. I know already that I'd like to open with Studs Terkel's *Working* this fall. I was at a public event in Houston in June at which one of the participants read an excerpt from it. The eloquence of the ordinary folk represented in it overwhelmed me anew. How much there is to learn about the rhythms of real speech from studying these interviews!

I'm partial to books that open out onto other vistas—literary, political, psychological. If we read *Great Expectations*, there's an opportunity to explore Victorian England. If it's *I Never Promised You a Rose Garden*, we can delve into mental illness and abnormal psychology. *Working* is ripe with possibilities in economics and sociology. There are a dozen ways to connect the reading to exciting writing activities and projects: students conducting interviews with parents and neighbors about their work; interviewing each other about their own job experiences; writing about their own work futures; doing research papers on issues relating to the job market, the workplace, unions, and so on; performing parts of the musical adaptation of *Working*. As I begin to see that I could spend the entire year on this one book, my senses tell me it's time to cut back, to accept reality and its attendant limitations.

On my first visit to my new school, my supervisor gave me copies of the syllabus for sophomore English and the textbook for that grade level. It's a good textbook, better than most, with more than the normal share of well-selected contemporary poetry and fiction alongside the old warhorses, nothing like that scripted teacher's guide I collided with in Vermont. I might even use it for a while at the beginning of the year until I get a sense of the level on which my students are operating. In general, I don't believe in textbooks for English students at any level. There are real books students can and should be reading regardless of age or ability. Textbooks will never produce literate adult readers. Only real books can accomplish that. Administrators often put their energies behind a uniform basal reader program for their schools when it's clear that even at the early grade levels, the way to promote reading is by exposing kids to the plethora of good books capable of exciting them about reading.

Another issue I'm wrestling with is how much reading to expect of students beyond the prescribed set of books we are exploring as a class. Students need to inhale great quantities of literature in their school years in order to get a reasonable sampling of the universe of inspired and inspiring writing they can choose from as independent adult readers. In my elementary and middle school classrooms, I evolved a program of independent reading that required students to read a certain number of books on their own and to document their reading in a variety of ways. What they read was a mix of books entirely of their own choosing and books they could choose from a long and varied list of classics I provided. In this system students read anywhere from ten to fifty books on their own over the course of the year.

There are flaws. All systems are vulnerable to cheating. Students can copy or adapt each other's written reports. They can resort to using *Cliffs Notes*, that time-honored sidekick for the harried, confused, and lazy student. Some students claim to hate the books they read under this kind of regime, simply because they are required to read them. Last year Howard, a student of stunning ingenuity, said to me after he finished the year's requirements, "You know, Dr. H, yesterday was the first day this year I really enjoyed reading a book. I was reading it even though I didn't have to, and I don't have to tell anyone about it." I remembered a similar moment I relished every year when the last exam was done and the final paper submitted; I could go to the library and attack the literature section with no accountability to anyone. In this imperfect world, however, resentment over being coerced into reading often masks unadmitted delight at new discoveries.

For example, Michael, a student at Rogers, chose to forgo written summaries in favor of taped monologues of his musings about his independent reading. On my late-afternoon jogs through the steamy streets of Houston, Michael's voice accompanied me as he marveled at the ways in which Robinson Crusoe's attempts to establish a life for himself recapitulated the history of human technological development or as he pondered why the seemingly structureless absurdity of *Catch-22* was so affecting. Mindy had rarely read a complete book on her own, an affliction she shared with some of my new high school students. For some reason, independent reading is rare at that level. Students are deemed too old for it, although the form of this particular demand does not seem age-bound to me.

Following a similarly misguided bit of developmental illogic, parents and teachers stop reading aloud to children when they seem reasonably equipped to read on their own. Yet people of all ages love to be read to, to be surrounded once again by that reassuring buzz that signals security, the suspension of all demands for performance. Nothing but attention is required. When older readers are given the proper alibi, they slip back into picture books of their prereading and early reading years with unconcealed delight. Reading experiences, like the observance of much religious ritual, is built on layers of childhood memories and associations that make traditional age boundaries far more fluid than we tend to think. At least that's the base from which I'd like to move my reading structure from the "younger" levels up into my high school class.

Since writing is always at the center of my classroom program, I have a lot of decisions to make about how I approach it next year. How much fiction and poetry versus so-called expository writing? How many structured assignments and how much free choice? How much writing will be done in class and how much at home? How can I connect the writing with the reading we'll be doing without falling into the classic high school trap of writing only about books? Do I want to convene editing groups that place heavy responsibility on students to critique each other's work, or do I want to retain more of that authority and responsibility for myself?

The questions proliferate and in the end become esoteric enough to interest only other teachers. With each question I am approximating my mechanic's reasoning as he follows the flow of electricity from my generator through the wires into the distributor cap and from there out to the individual spark plugs. One doesn't need to know how it works in the same detail that he has mastered, but it certainly is intriguing to watch him puzzle it all out.

Why trouble anyone else with all these seemingly endless issues of book selection, independent reading systems, choice of writing assignments? As the auto mechanic understands, it's all this little stuff that keeps the car moving down the road. In school, each of the nuts and bolts decisions I am pondering for next year contains implicit within it numerous assumptions and conclusions about education, about our culture, about children and how they develop and learn, and about the role of teachers in a student's learning. Choosing new books to read each year and trying to distribute them into the various categories I've described presupposes that there is a vast body of literature worthy of being brought before the students. We can sample from it without assuming that there are specific fixtures in the cultural firmament that all students must encounter at a specific time.

Providing a good education means attuning students to the fact that there are a richness and diversity of cultures, experiences, and styles that await, ready to yield themselves up to whoever chooses to partake. Although former education secretary William Bennett may disagree, white students need to know of Ralph Ellison and Toni Morrison as much as black students should experience Dickens and Edith Wharton. This diversity cannot be communicated by cleaving too closely to what is comfortable and familiar; we have an obligation to stretch and extend students beyond the level on which they come to us.

My teenage reading years predated the era of juvenile and young adult fiction. This intriguing form can run the spectrum from masterful art to unspeakable drivel. (Come to think of it, one can say precisely the same for adult fiction.) In its absence I read trashy adult novels—more accurately, sections of them—sports histories and biographies, and I began to explore the adult bookshelves earlier than I otherwise might have. Today I would pit writers like Cynthia Voigt, Katherine Patterson, Virginia Hamilton, Robert Cormier, and Zibby Oneal against most writers of adult fiction, but I have become aware that the genre as a whole creates some unanticipated problems for me as a teacher and for my students as readers. Once students are fed on the bouncing first-person colloquial of Judy Blume and her many imitators, whose voices mesh seamlessly with those of their readers, they have little tolerance for an unfamiliar voice, an embellished vocabulary, an alien style. Students are all too often irritated by language different in any way from what washes around them every day. Similarly, boys have become immersed in the extensive fantasy literature that has taken particular hold in the years since the advent of Dungeons and Dragons—a rich, open-ended game that pits knights and wizards and dragons against each other. (As an astute ten-year-old once explained to me, "Oh, it's great. You can get rich, have power, and kill.") Although fantasy literature at its best can be imaginative and entertaining, it is short on characterization and detail and long on action. It's true that adventure books like *Tom Swift* have been around for several generations, but not in the present quantities and not for an increasingly older readership.

The net effect of the proliferation of juvenile and young adult fiction is to reduce students' tolerance for reading cloaked in unfamiliar styles, spun out in denser detail, or following unfamiliar characters. Children are the world's true conservatives. They want exactly what they've already had. Dickens and Shakespeare are weird. *The Sound and the Fury* and *Death of a Salesman*, although they're more contemporary, are also weird because of their nonlinear structures. A few daring young adult writers like Robert Cormier have experimented with forms like these, but students are generally programmed to expect lockstep chronological writing. Thus do we create the consumers of blockbuster airport novels.

There's no way around Shakespeare, although few dare to try it before the high school years. But in our earnest and well-intentioned efforts to motivate students by choosing work that they can relate to with a minimum of effort, we have narrowed our choices so that we all appear to be hungry flies feeding off the same tasty morsel of meat. The books we choose to teach from are adult books that resemble as closely as possible the Young Adult and juvenile novels our students prefer. *Catcher in the Rye* and *A Separate Peace* are outstanding books everyone should read, but how to explain the fact that they have achieved a universality in schools that is rivaled only by Shakespeare? Obviously, the protagonists are of approximately the same age as the readers, and the language, particularly Salinger's, goes down easy. Although Holden Caulfield speaks in the cadences of a 1950s teenager, his voice seems as timeless as 1960s Beatles music to contemporary adolescent listeners. Surely the arsenal of literature extends more broadly than this and includes works of nonfiction, works from other countries and cultures. Check out middle school and high school reading lists. You will be hard pressed to find works that aren't American or British, and forms other than plays or novels. The neglect of poetry, particularly contemporary poetry, is a tragedy of epic proportions, and it goes a long way toward explaining the virtual nonexistence of any adult poetry readership in this country.

I have studied Shakespeare and Dickens with my middle school students. I am not alone in this. My friend Phillip Lopate, the gifted writer and teacher, has performed and studied Chekhov with sixth graders. I recently sat through a perfectly serviceable performance of *Macbeth* by a group of third, fourth, and fifth graders who clearly understood the lines they were delivering—and took pleasure in them. It's a stretch that requires resourcefulness on the part of the teacher and a willingness to fight through the initial resistance born of unfamiliarity. Teachers who want to be loved by every student at every moment will shy away from the tasks that elicit groans. "Oh God, not poetry!" (Or substitute for poetry Shakespeare or Dickens.)

Jerome Bruner said that students of any age can learn any subject matter, provided it is presented in the right way. A bit of hyperbole, perhaps, but not too far from what I believe and have seen. Let's take Shakespeare, for example. For years I opened my study of one or another of Shakespeare's plays with the aid of a troupe of student actors from the University of Houston, led by Professor Rutherford Cravens.

Ruddy enters the classroom. He is bespectacled, wears a tan tie and tweed jacket, a professor's professor. As he proceeds to lecture on some esoteric aspect of Shakespeare, several of his actors who are planted in the audience begin to complain loudly about how boring the presentation is. An angry confrontation between professor and audience moves from shoutdown to swords, and the performers are off spouting lines of Shakespeare at one another. For a time the audience is stunned by the display of raw emotion rarely seen in school, but once they recognize that it's all part of the performance, they settle in to enjoy what follows: a series from *Romeo and Juliet, Taming of the Shrew,* and *Midsummer Night's Dream*, all carefully chosen to show Shakespeare at his bawdiest and most amusingly irreverent. Once the students have seen Kate and Petruchio exchange sexually charged barbs right there in their own classroom, I never have trouble convincing them that a struggle with the mysterious Elizabethan language might yield some surprising results.

I own a complete collection of my school's literary magazines, which I treasure as much as some of my students treasure their comic book and baseball card collections. Every year at reunion time I flip back through them, forever the diligent student, in a futile attempt to avoid the embarrassment of meeting kids whose names have become disconnected from their faces in my mind. Inevitably, I am drawn to the scrawled inscriptions inside the front and back covers: the joking jabs at my baldness; the purposely error-studded tribute to my superlative teaching (YEW HAS BIN MY MOST BEST GRAMMUR TECHUR); the sincere but embarrassing testimonials to the best English teacher they ever had. But the ones I really cherish and return to for moral support are those that admit to early anger and irritation at the demands I made— the quantity of writing and reading, and the level of reading (Shakespeare and Dickens). There are a few of these in each literary magazine, and they always end with an acknowledgment of the satisfaction the writers feel at having accomplished something difficult. They have surprised themselves, the best form of self-discovery. It is a validation of the teacher's obligation to expect a lot of students. No pep talks are required. The expectations are implicit in the work being asked of students and in the tone and manner in which one addresses them. I'm sure there are kids who left my class cursing the bad luck that had brought them there, but I think most kids recognize and respect hard work that is honest and draw the proper distinction between mind-numbing answers to chapter questions and reading and writing that allow freshness and surprise.

We have drifted into the deep and murky waters of expectations of students and the very composition of our culture. And we have arrived there via the most mundane of routes: by looking at the seemingly humdrum issues of how to set up a classroom reading program. I had good mentors in the sixties and later, philosopher-practitioners who taught me well that every seemingly trivial decision and choice in the life of an institution or individual has philosophical implications against which it must be measured. Who designs and orders materials for the Head Start playground indicates where the real versus the nominal power lies and how serious those above are about sharing that power. The amount of money this school district's staff development committee allocates to reimburse teachers for taking college courses as opposed to releasing them to meet with their colleagues to develop new curriculum embodies a philosophy of how teachers learn and grow and how they translate that growth to benefit children.

So looking over a teacher's shoulder to observe his planning process not only satisfies a legitimate voyeuristic interest, but also enables us to look at deeper questions of what schools are trying to accomplish and why they are succeeding or failing.

Sprinting Houston garbagemen, my mechanic in his oil-stained small-town garage, a teacher at his summer planning desk—they are all attempting to navigate a course through their work that is mindful, that represents their best thinking about the way things should be done. That is craft.

The more experienced you become, the more you internalize the basic structure, so that you expend minimal energy on how to keep things moving in class, the mechanics of scheduling assignments, keeping control, starting and ending a lesson. There's a slow accretion of techniques and tricks, a backlog of materials, units, lessons, and ideas that you have faith in and don't have to reinvent each time. It's around this basic framework that the artistry of the teacher, like the artistry of the jazz musician, can take flight.

I find myself drawn repeatedly to analogy between good teaching and jazz. The kind of jazz I love has a discernible shape and structure around which the musician can coil riffs and variations as the spirit moves him. He may not know exactly where he is headed when he steps off the prescribed track, and he may never wind up in the same place twice in a row. What emerges may not always be beautiful, but the process is going to be interesting to both the listener and the performer; a bond of curiosity will link player and audience to each other and to the music.

I was ill prepared for my first teaching job in a fifth and sixth grade classroom. In a frenzy of anxiety, I carted home the dead weight of textbooks I was apparently responsible for covering, along with their even bulkier teachers' guides. These were the real shockers, not guides at all, but out and out scripts, complete with stage directions:

> Now say, "Children, what do you notice about the punctuation in the first line in this story?" (Pause for response.)
> Then respond, "That's right. It's in quotation marks. Can anyone say why that is?"

This was teaching as technology, built on the assumption that somehow we could transcend the shortcomings of the individual teacher by fashioning the perfect set of materials and methods that any dolt could use successfully.

During the fortunate times when I am pleased with what is happening in my classroom, I am acting more as the artist than as the technician. Although successful teaching involves elements of both, futile attempts to eliminate failure and risk produce only sterility. It is the risks, the potential for embarrassing flops, the unpredictability that generate the excitement that accompanies real learning.

We are asking the student to bring his or her whole being to us, and we in turn must do the same, imperfections, failures, and all. In *How to Survive in Your Native Land*, the late teacher and author James Herndon spoke of the necessity of teachers toppling the barriers between their lives in and out of school, to inhabit

> your classroom like a human being instead of playing some idiot role which everyone knows is a role, time to see that teaching . . . is connected with your life and with you as a human being, citizen, person, that you don't have to become something different like a Martian or an idiot for eight hours a day.

Good teaching is an odd mix of artistry, vulnerability, and technical prowess. We reach down into our own interests and experience to sketch our plans; we fall short of our vision, back up and try a new path through the underbrush; we listen to what students, colleagues, parents have to say about our work and use those observations to devise yet another set of strategies.

In pursuing our elevated goals, we try to avoid the cardinal sin of being boring. We must lighten the burden of those fifty-minute slabs of gray stone into which the school day is divided, lest we be buried by them and become the subjects of these painful lines I ran across years ago by Randall Jarrell (I wish I had recorded the title of the book from which I lifted them, but I've had no luck relocating the source):

My teachers could have rode
with Jesse James
So many were the hours
they stole from me.

CHAPTER 7

Four Days

In early March, Kristen gave me a draft of the short story she had chosen to do for her writing contract. Although she had been reading it to her writing group, she wanted my comments. It was an astonishingly well written piece, full of rich complex sentences and good metaphor. But the story itself was straight out of the romance novels. Two girls, best of friends since one was adopted by the other's parents after a tragedy in her own family, are driven apart by a young man. Girl #1 falls in love with him. Girl #2, in jealousy, makes a play and steals him away. Girl #1 in despair destroys herself in a car wreck. Story ends with Girl #2 delivering a guilt-ridden soliloquy at #1's graveside.

In my comments, I praised Kristen's writing and her story-telling ability, but I tried to explain that all this melodrama wasn't necessary to make a good story. Smaller, more subtle things could happen. Characters could change in more internal ways; they didn't have to wreck themselves in a flaming accident. Several times over the next few weeks, Kristen stopped me to say that she was struggling with the revision, but she was trying to respond to what I had suggested. The hardest thing to get across to kids at this stage in the writing process is that I am making *suggestions*; I am *not* instructing them about what they are to do. The story is theirs. They need to listen hard to what I and their other readers say in response to their work, but they are the owners of what they create and must make the final decisions. This is a tricky reversal of authority and student-teacher power relations, one for which kids have no previous model. "I'm supposed to change the ending?" is the usual response.

Kristen is a very compliant young woman, and that's the direction she was headed until the night before her conference with me. She was finishing up her independent reading requirement by reading *Death Be Not Proud*, John Gunther's chronicle of his son's death from a brain tumor. The book made her angry. He was dealing with the whole experience in such a measured, dispassionate way. Where was the grief, the sorrow? She couldn't feel anything because Gunther didn't seem to be allowing himself to feel anything.

In one of those wonderful, unaccountable leaps, Kristen connected her own story with Gunther's. She decided that her story was cold too, when what she most wanted was to move the reader. Her story was told by a narrator, a distant third-person voice that kept the reader far from the characters. (I'm paraphrasing her words, but not much.) So she had sat down last night and tried an experiment. She had taken one of her girls and placed her in a mental institution. She was now telling the story, all of the events that led to her breakdown. It felt altogether different in the mouth of this character. There was more feeling. But the problem was that her contract was up and she needed to turn the story in.

I was awestruck. Kristen had made a literary discovery on her own that was beyond the reach of a lot of adult writers: the significance of voice and point of view in fiction and the ways in which the final product is shaped by the choice of who tells the story. I once heard an interview with a novelist (I think it was Ed McLanahan) who described laboring over a novel for many years before he realized the wrong person was telling the story. Contract? Who cares about that? Go home and pursue your discovery. These school requirements take on a reality of their own for the kids and teachers so that they obscure the true objective, which in this case is to stimulate the best possible writing. Kristen was actually grateful to be "liberated" to do all this extra work on her story. I'm the one who's grateful for the gift she gave both of us in this otherwise gloomy week.

There were two other small gifts that week in the form of reading journals that students produced for independent reading. Vanessa had read *Siddhartha*, which I would have imagined to be the least appropriate book on the list for her, but it was skinny and I had assigned it double credit as an inducement for students to read it. Vanessa is so concrete and literal minded that for her this account of a philosophical quest was as appropriate as a Perrier for a rodeo rider.

And here came Vanessa with an eight-page journal full of insights about the parallels between Siddhartha's quest and her own aspirations for perfection and wholeness through her gymnastics, about parallels between her relationship with her mother and some of Siddhartha's relationships, and so on. Only the week before, Vanessa had turned in the third draft of a god-awful piece of writing about Freedom (with a capital F) that I had tried every way I knew how to warn her off: "Write about what you know." But she had decided she wanted to write something "important," the result of which was a mishmash of anticommunism and tirades against poverty, hijacking, and censorship. With the praise she got for the reading journal, the message finally came across: You really can address big issues—if you start from yourself. She decided that for her next writing project she wanted to write about her two gymnastics teachers and how their ways of dealing with her elicited different performances from her.

Cary read *The Chosen* straight through, then decided to reread it and produce her journal the second time around. It was a piece of work so elaborate and ambitious that it was out of all proportion to the requirements of the assignment. Some kids overproduce in response to an internalized insistence on perfection; some do it as a manifestation of over-compliance. In Cary's case, I think she had a crush on her bald old teacher and was trying to win my attention and praise through her work. This is one of the undiscussed issues of teaching—the student-teacher "transference" and all the sexual undercurrents that can swirl around it. Even in middle school I watched a gay colleague do noble battle with a mutual attraction involving a particularly mature and forward young man in his class. I am calculating enough to be able to exploit Cary's innocent mooning by transforming it into motivating energy to produce the best work she's capable of.

This week of wonderful individual efforts and break-throughs was also the week of those ubiquitous achieve-ment tests we assault our students with every year. Even for the superb test takers, the process exacts its toll in anxiety and strain. This year, for the first time, principal and admin-istration were being evaluated on the basis of their school's test scores, a logical extension of certain aspects of account-ability but one with potentially disastrous implications for education. First, it defines the goals of teaching and educa-tion in an unacceptably narrow way (the content of the test is what should be taught). Second, it opens up the possibility of abuse by overzealous administrators who are going to beat up on kids to make the adults look good. The principal visited all the classes to tell them how important these tests were and to encourage them to do their very best.

Needless to say, she didn't tell them what she had riding on the results.

During testing week, so much goes into a holding pattern. We're discouraged from doing anything too intense. Kids need to be rested and fit for the tests. We mustn't distract them unduly with schoolwork. See the travesty of a handout that was sent home with all the kids when I was teaching middle school:

An Open Letter From Iowa

Hi there!

I'm the Basic Skills Test from the Corn State of Iowa. I go here and there every year to see just how much my friends have grown mentally. I make you a "V.I.P." by comparing your performance with other students of the same age and grade throughout the country.

More about me, huh? Well, I'm divided in eleven separately timed tests which cover a wide range of skills—vocabulary, reading, mechanics of writing, methods of study and mathematics. I'm different from the average test you might have met because only my correct answers count and I don't hold the wrong ones against you.

Hold on there, now . . . Don't get uptight about me because you will not fail me. But on the other hand, do your very best, for you can use my results as one measure of where you are going educationally and the best way to get there. I can help you make realistic educational and career plans. I can predict with some degree of accuracy those subject areas in which you will be weak or strong.

I come fully equipped with the latest in answer sheets for recording your responses. Although I'm considered a long test, I'm really worth your time. Get a good night's sleep the night before the test. Bring several sharpened pencils and an eraser to the test session. I'm looking forward to working with you real soon.

Basically yours,
Iowa Test of Basic Skills

It was March. I was tired and I knew from bitter experience that a string of interruptions and disruptions stretched out from here to June with little relief. The impulse is to drift into port with the engine barely turning over.

Yet it is precisely at these times that one must push against the inertia. Because my energy was low, I needed to hit upon a final major project that would help focus me and the kids productively. I didn't know yet what the project would be, but I knew it would center around either or both of the last two books: *The Autobiography of Miss Jane Pittman* and *Night*—black history and World War II. I remember the wonderful principal in Peacham, Vermont, who dealt with year-end slump by giving out report cards a month early, declaring the "formal" part of school over, and plunging everyone in a schoolwide town history, Foxfire-type project. Most of the kids worked a lot harder than they did in their regular classes, but they didn't define it as work. I didn't have the solution yet, but I knew it would come to me.

I am deeply skeptical about the efficacy of teaching grammar as a separate entity divorced from student writing. Nevertheless, I've continued to do it. That week we finished a chapter on complex sentences, and a vast number of kids did terribly on the test. There was massive anxiety, frustration, and anger. I was irritated with myself for not getting the material across better and angry with the kids for being too obtuse to grasp the concepts. "Are you mad at me?" one perceptive student asked as we were going over the test. Embarrassed, I denied it, but the truth is I was angry at all of us and ultimately at the need to do this at all.

Why am I doing this? I asked myself. My goal is to enable students to write correctly and comfortably. There's lots of evidence to show that these skills bear no relation to formal grammar instruction. I have to conclude that I'm doing it for noninstructional reasons—to make my class look legitimate, to ward off parent criticism, and so forth. I can't do that anymore.

I decided that the only grammar I would teach must bear some connection to writing. I was swearing off and I had to tell the kids why, being careful not to do any grandstanding for student praise here, since the decision would clearly be a popular one.

On Tuesday of that week, we were studying the first act of *Othello*. The discussion centered on Iago's pathological jealousy and paranoia. As evidence for this I focused on "And it is thought abroad that 'twixt my sheets [Othello] has done my office."

"Anybody understand that?" Blank. So I start taking it apart. What does *'twixt* mean? If *office* is understood as a duty or a job, what now?

"Oh, I get it," shouts Carol from the back of the room and starts cackling loudly. She explains to her tablemate the sexual connotations as she scribbles in her book the interpretation she has grasped.

"Hey, this stuff would be terrific," she says, "if it was in English."

I work harder on teaching Shakespeare than on just about anything I do all year. Because it's such a struggle for kids, I have to meet them more than halfway, not just with good teaching devices, but with far more physical energy than is my normal style. I'm usually fairly low-key, calm, earnest, and serious. Whatever response I elicit from the kids is less a reflection of showmanship than it is a product of a relaxed, supportive, clear, and well-organized environment in which kids are given work they like to do (compared to schoolwork), are treated respectfully, and know what's expected of them. It's not a flamboyant, high-energy performance. Much as I would like to provide that and much as I recognize the need for it with kids this age whose attention otherwise seems to migrate back into their midbrains, it's just not my style. You play the instrument you're given, and mine is mellow and muted. It appeals to certain sensitive, introspective kids who are, in fact, very much like me, but not as much to the kids whose threshold of attention is higher.

Teacher-student relationships are like marriages. Various sets of partners are compatible to varying degrees. When the pieces don't mesh well, it's not necessarily a reflection on either partner. The neurotic need that some teachers have for every student to love them cannot be satisfied. I'm sure there are kids who, even if they like me, think I'm a dull teacher. That's the analogue of dating a girl whom you damn with faint praise by declaring her "nice."

The point is that Shakespeare encourages me to reach down a little deeper toward some other source of vitality. The day of the Shakespeare lesson was one of the rare days when I had to drag myself off to school. I had slept badly the night before. In addition, a Mexican dinner was not sitting well in my stomach. I mention these details only because they're such rare occurrences for me. My morning mood has always been a measure of the rightness of my work life. I can count on the fingers of one hand the number of days when I've awakened dreading what lay ahead. During the one brief period when my seven A.M. body and psyche began sending out warning signals I knew it was time for me to leave my job at Antioch. I acted on it quickly and all was calm again.

The day before, Norma Klein, a well-known young adult writer and an old friend who has since died, had been in to talk to my class. Among other things, she described her incredibly mechanical procedure of writing ten pages day in, day out, with little revision, until her book is done (a month for a juvenile book!). Much as this process makes me shudder, there is one important constructive message in it. Norma said, "I force myself to write those ten pages no matter what mood I'm in. I haven't noticed that there's any difference in the quality of what I write when I feel great and when I feel lousy."

Sure enough, puffy eyes, rebellious bowels, and all, I did some of my best teaching that day. I led kids through Acts II and III of *Othello*. I paced, I gesticulated, I discussed ideas and connections I hadn't noticed before. Suddenly, I was expanding on the idea of Iago as a master chess player, capable of thinking many steps ahead of stratagems to ensnare and undo his unwitting victims. I searched out all the ribaldry—the anal and sexual humor. What adolescent can resist the idea that when Shakespeare's clown prattles on about wind instruments, he's referring to body functions as well as trumpets? By the time my fifth-period class came in, they all knew I had used the word *fart* in my earlier classes. A sure-fire advertisement for Shakespeare!

One day during the break between sixth and seventh period, Jan came into my room to ask if she could see me in her office. When we got down there and closed the door behind us, I asked what was up.

"I have no idea. The kids asked me to keep you busy for a while." Since it wasn't my birthday and I hadn't won any awards, I couldn't imagine what they had up their collective sleeves.

Jan went back to determine whether the coast was clear and reported that they were more than ready, and in fact had taken her to task for keeping me too long. When I opened the door, the lights were out and everyone burst forth from under the table shouting "Congratulations!" Adam appeared from the book room with a cake inscribed "Congredulations, Dr. Hoffman" ("Those people at Randall's can't even spell," exclaims Adam, who's no great shakes with the consonants himself) and featuring a great big orange basketball. And therein lies the tale.

Two days earlier we had had our faculty-student basketball game during lunch period. That's a misnomer, since the basketball coach and I were the only official faculty members participating. The rest of the team was patched together from aides and janitorial and maintenance staff people. We had actually practiced together for two days after school. Although there was a good crowd of students in the stands, you knew what a low-priority activity this was for the school as a whole when the fire drill bell rang during warm-ups and we were all forced to evacuate the building, thus cutting into our actual playing time.

The students beat us in this abbreviated game, eighteen to twelve, but I accounted for half our team's points with two baskets and one assist. It's such a minor event in the flow of school activities, but it raises some interesting issues to ponder.

First, the response I got from the students was amazing. In addition to the surprise party I've already described, on the afternoon after the game, when I returned to class, still sweaty and unshowered, I got a standing ovation. Students stopped me in the hall for the next two days to comment on my prowess on the court. Partly it's the sense of surprise that this bald old man not only could manage to run up and down the court without keeling over but could actually handle himself with some skill.

The important thing is that the kids got to see me in a role and context different from the one in which they encounter me every day. I think it's enormously important for everyone to be able to see the people in their lives acting in many different roles. One of the prime virtues of small-town life resides in the fact that you meet up with everyone in multiple roles: your plumber is also your selectman and a parent of a kid in your class and a teammate in the local slow-pitch baseball league. Dealing with people in only one arena of their lives (usually the professional) discourages the kind of textured and compassionate interaction with them that grows out of a more complex recognition that standing before you is a mass of overlapping and virtually irreconcilable roles, all too human in his or her vulnerabilities and ambitions.

Nowhere are the pitfalls of this one-dimensional relationship more evident than in schools. Remember the old fantasy kids have that their teachers live in the school and sleep on their desks at night because they can't imagine them in any other role than teacher. I think it's a tremendous boon for a teacher to be perceived by the kids also as a parent, a husband or wife, a sports fan, a weekend carpenter, whatever. It makes them more receptive to you, more forgiving of your foibles and more understanding of your style.

Let's not forget that it's a two-way street, too. After the basketball game, one of the teachers said about a student, "Alex was a whole different person out there on the basketball court than he is in class. I never dreamed he could do some of the things he did." So often we see our kids only in their role as student and forget what a small part of their lives that is and how many other dimensions to their behavior we're not seeing. Hoffman the basketball player/teacher and Alex the basketball player/student met in a different arena, and I can't help thinking that their relationship in the classroom will be better for it, particularly when I'm tossing some Shakespeare at him and he's asking himself what kind of person would be interested in this stuff.

Test taking is one thing, using your body another. One of the hidden benefits of being a teacher is that you get a second shot at certain aspects of your childhood. You can relive some of the triumphs and repair some of the failures. I had

experienced the joys of teaching elementary school kids
in an activity-centered classroom where I was able to experiment with making and building things, learning through
physical experience after a childhood in which learning
was almost strictly verbal. The same kid who used to beg his
mother to let him stay home on the days the teacher was
going to do weaving during art period took great pleasure as
an adult teacher leafing through *Weaving without a Loom*,
or mastering techniques of silk-screening, electrical wiring,
plaster casting, and furniture building. It's the Second
Coming! Michael Jordan and this benchwarmer get another
chance to demonstrate our prowess on the basketball court.

CHAPTER 8

Working:
Trying on New Roles

Much of what we plan as teachers gets jettisoned or modified beyond recognition. My summertime vision of finding a place for Studs Terkel's *Working* was a rare survivor, as a year-end project, in spite of considerable guilt that some significant work from the canon—*Walden, Huck Finn, Gatsby, Farewell to Arms*—would have to be bumped to make room for it. It does not sit easy on the conscience of any serious English teacher to turn students loose on the world with those kinds of gaps in their learning. But it's a delusion to think that one can make even the best of students completely literate in 180 class hours, so there's no harm in one deviation from the sacred works of fiction. I am hardly the first to use *Working* in a high school classroom. Some of the censorship battles surrounding the book have been well publicized, including Terkel's own personal appearance before a Pennsylvania school board to defend the use of his book in the curriculum. His attackers appeared to be offended by the fact that real people use nasty words in their daily conversations, and Terkel was unwilling to sanitize that fact out of existence. I had no information on how the book had actually been used, so I was on my own in designing an approach to *Working*. All I had to go on was my intuition that students would be as charmed by these honest, lusty, hopeful, and cynical voices as I had been and that the issues of how people spend their work lives would engage them. High school sophomores in a fairly high achieving magnet program are already extremely preoccupied with their own work futures, perhaps to a fault. Kids are pestered from an early age to declare themselves on their future professions. They must do this on woefully inadequate information, since most jobs in the adult work world stand outside children's line of vision. How many of them have considered the life of a Coast Guard crew member or a hotel troubleshooter or the manager of a costume shop, yet all three of these jobs are held by people whom my students subsequently interviewed. Even in the seemingly more familiar jobs—lawyer, doctor, research scientist—most of us have little sense of the actual texture of the day-to-day work lives that lie concealed behind these labels.

What specific knowledge about work have young people accumulated from the laboratory of their own lives? For better or worse, most high school students have part-time jobs. (The definition of part time becomes obscured when I discover from a student who has been dozing in class that he worked the four-to-midnight shift last night in a food-supply warehouse and that he does this six days a week.) It is a rare student who has not held down a summer job or who has not worked at baby-sitting. In-class opportunities to address this aspect of students' lives are rare despite the fact that it is often more vivid and absorbing than what transpires between period bells. In addition, students are simultaneously observers, victims, and beneficiaries of their parents' work lives, continually assessing the merits and drawbacks of their work choices, taking seismic readings of parental moods at the end of the workday, even in the surprisingly frequent situations in which they have little real knowledge of what their parents *do* at work. Among my "regular" students, where unemployment and underemployment are more common than in the upwardly mobile families of the Vanguard students, attitudes toward work—present and future—would surely take on a different cast.

We began our *Working* project by reading together Terkel's three prefatory sections of memorable interviews. These raised questions that became the leitmotivs for many of our subsequent discussions: money versus meaning in the choice of work; the impulse to leave a visible and lasting mark on the world; the unjust and reductionist stereotypes with which most jobs are weighed. Simultaneous with our reading of the prefaces, I asked the students to write about their own visions of their personal work futures: What do you see yourself doing ten to fifteen years from now? Why did you choose this particular direction? Who influenced you? How do your dreams for yourself match your parents' dreams for you? How do you feel about your parents' work lives—the choices they have made, the satisfaction they get? Where are you on the issue of money versus meaning? Is there someone who is your idol—a person whose work life comes closest to what you'd like yours to be?

> By the year 2003, I can picture myself bent over with the sun shining on the back of my long, reddened neck. I will be working with my bony but strong fingers. Natives of the land will surround me, also busy with the newly planted crops. I will be able to feel the hot brown earth between my toes and the sturdy bridge beneath my feet. . . . My work would be of an engineering type closely knit with the skill of farming. . . . This kind of work would give me great internal and mental satisfaction. I feel useless till somebody needs my help. (Alyson)

Lately I've been thinking that I might try teaching. This may come from the fact that both my parents are teachers or that some of the more influential people in my life have been or are teachers.

I think from my tentative career choice it becomes obvious that money really isn't all that important to me. Teachers just don't make that much money. I think I'm lucky because I came from a home that never had a lot of money and never really missed it. . . . My inspiration in this regard comes from my folks. Both love to teach, love their kids and both seem self-fulfilled. (Jeremy)

I feel strongly that I would rather work at a job where I enjoy myself and made less money than a job I hated and made more money. To me money isn't everything. It can buy some things that make you happy, but look what you have to do to get it. Suffering day after day at a boring job just isn't worth it. (Darrell)

I hate to say it, but I come out on the money side of the balance. Of course helping people will be important, but never as important as money. (Tiffany)

I feel sorry for my parents in their jobs. My dad was a history major, went into the business world and now has a very stressful position. My mom wanted to be a marine biologist, but she also went into the business world. They are both under a lot of stress. I think they work because they must. (Toby)

My parents are not satisfied with their jobs at all. My mother is a housewife, while my stepfather is a truck driver. They are both always tired. . . . They sit on their butts and just complain all the time and say, "We want better for you all. . . ." They're really two lost souls. . . . There's no meaning and especially no money in either job. (Terry)

The heart of the *Working* project lay in the interviews the students conducted. Terkel's results don't come automatically. There is an art to questioning, the kind open-ended enough to encourage expansive responses rather than the lockjaw, monosyllabic answers that drive interviewers to despair. I modeled an interview in class, questioning a student about his own work experience. Then the students paired off and interviewed each other about their jobs. From the notes of these sessions, they wrote up the interviews in the style of Terkel's book, portions of which they had been assigned to read. I encouraged them to follow his lead in editing themselves out of the interview, leaving something as close to a seamless monologue as possible. Always the exhortation was to try to capture on paper as much of the speaker's real voice as possible.

I remember one summer when I used to babysit for money. . . . The father always came and picked me up even though I lived right down the street. He had this ruddy face that made me really nervous. I'm not sure he ever noticed it, but I used to hold an open knife in my left hand real tight on the outside of my left leg facing him. With my right hand I held the door, always expecting him to turn a different way and take me somewhere. I was always ready to make a run for it. (Kate by Alyson)

I was a file clerk working with my sister in an attorney's office. The lawyers worked for these stores like Montgomery Ward, Highland, Levitz Furniture. The job was to check creditors and see who was paying. If they were not paying they would take their stuff. One time there was this man that wasn't paying back the money he owed and they took back everything, from his TV and microwave to his dog. (Laughs) And I ask the boss, "You took the man's dog?" The man said, "Can't pay, can't stay!" (Sherena by Terry)

(On working at the zoo)
I also unload produce for the animals, lots of dog food. Dog food has got enough of the nutritional value that many animals need. We also unload and bring in huge boxes of crickets. The box screens have millions of dead crickets.

They're gross because they're all smushed and their legs fall off. Most of the volunteers are girls, but they'd rather have guys because they expect guys to do heavier work. They respect guys more, but guys don't do much. I'm offended by that. (Dawnelle by Becky)

With these in-class interviews under their belts, the students set out to do a more extended interview with an adult whom they admired or about whose work they were curious. I asked them to inform me ahead of time about their interview plans, mainly as a spur to get them to think ahead about who might make an interesting subject. I almost never needed to veto their choices. A number of interviews were with family members, which always yield the side benefit of increasing communication at home, opening up for discussion hitherto unaired issues. The range of jobs in these interviews was impressive: cantor, licensed vocational nurse, television newscaster, shoe salesclerk, automobile window tinter.

Anthony Villareal, power company troubleshooter
During Hurricane Alicia, I worked fourteen hours a day, seven days a week. That's how it was for two weeks. In Alicia we had more people without power than we had customers during Hurricane Carla in the '60s. There were good people in the field that worked hard and long hours. People got their lights on in a reasonable amount of time. Now the only thing they think about is how much they pay.

I get to bring home all the electricity I can put in my pockets. I'm a rate payer like everyone else. Our motto is "Service First." I believe we are true to that. We're professionals. (Tina)

Maria Vela, employee at exclusive hotel
See, the restaurant is so private that people go there from all over the world. They find that the club is one of the few

places they can go to and not be bothered by everyone. Our customers have privacy and they enjoy the peace. I've met kings, queens, actresses, actors and all sorts of important people. They stay at the hotel and have lunch at the club. Every day I deal with the same kind of people. We can't get excited so that they are disturbed. That's got to be the hardest part of all. Here we have all these interesting, famous and important people coming in and out, but we have to act normal as if to us it was no big deal. (Cindy)

Charles Buchanan, trash collector
Sometimes people don't realize what they're throwing away or don't care. I've found many rings that are not cheap. I found one ring that had a diamond on each side of an opal stone. The ring band was gold. I took it to a jeweler and he said it was worth $250. I still have that ring. Sunday is my only day off. I don't do anything much but watch TV with my good buddy, "Jack Daniels." I'm not married and I don't have children nagging me to do things. My money is my own and no one else's. When Sunday's gone, so's my weekend and everything else starts all over again. (Tiffany D.)

Bonnie Ambrose, costume shop owner
We had somebody call up one day who wanted to rent a steer costume. And, yeah, well, we do have a steer cos-tume, and your face is exposed, but it has big steer horns and a steer nose and it's kind of, you know, kind of a funny thing. They said, "Well, what size is it?" And I said, "Oh, well, it'll fit a man up to a suit size 44 and it has big feet and all this." And finally the guy said, "Well, can it drive a truck?" (Laughs) He wanted to use it in a commercial. It made us laugh. (Melanie)

Elton Ray Washington, coast guardsman
A couple of hours earlier we received a call that a child needed to be transported across the bridge to Galveston hospital. Since the bridge was closed, they needed a boat to take her. We got this call. When we got to the scene of the car accident, the doctors there told us the baby would

die if we didn't get her across to Galveston quickly. We got her aboard and headed across. We went as fast as we could. When we got to Galveston, an ambulance was waiting. We gave the paramedics the child. They just stood there. We asked what was keeping them. They said it was too late, the child had died. After that all of us were depressed. (Darrell)

Although the interviews had been done individually outside of class, the students had also been divided into teams of four or five to carry out other parts of the project. Because the full text of *Working* runs 756 pages, far too long for cover-to-cover reading, each of the groups chose different sections to read, averaging 150 to 200 pages. For each interview in their assigned section, students completed an index card on which they recorded a favorite quote, some observations about the satisfactions and dissatisfactions the person seemed to experience from the job, and notes about the ways in which this person deviated from the stereotype often associated with that occupation.

The groups met several times to compare notes on their characters, to choose their favorites and to weave together from the words of these favorites, dramatic scenes that highlighted their characters' personalities and voices. Here we had as our model the adaptation of *Working* by Stephen Schwartz and Nina Faso, which brought to the stage in a musical version some of the most memorable of Terkel's characters. We had done dramatic readings (minus the songs, which are beyond my tone-deaf capacity) from the script, and the students then proceeded to stage their own newly crafted scenes. The stage work and the central focus on voice and character provided a wonderful transition to an extended play-reading and playwriting project that succeeded our six-week immersion in *Working*.

Terkel's style and subject matter led us off into some side

excursions that don't fit neatly into traditional lesson plans but are the stuff of exciting learning. Walt Whitman seemed to be speaking to us from behind Terkel's panoramic celebration of the American Everyone, so we detoured for several days to read from *Leaves of Grass* and to try our hand at writing poetry in the style of Whitman.

There were other roads not taken as time ran out. I had hoped to have students choose work-related research projects: teenagers, work, and school; women in the job market; the decline of industrial jobs; minority unemployment; and the like. We never got to it. Nor did we get to the supplementary reading list of novels and short fiction that touch on the lives of people at work. The canon was calling, and we had to content ourselves with a wrap-up that involved the students pulling together their interviews, monologues, personal work futures, Whitman imitations, and other short, in-class writing assignments into an anthology called *Working Papers*. It was on the basis of this compilation that they received their grade for the project.

I conduct a postmortem evaluation on virtually every extended activity we do in class. The reviews of the *Working* project were overwhelmingly positive. Students said they enjoyed the reading, the group discussions centered on their note cards, the dramatic opportunities, and the chance to learn something about interviewing. The greatest bonus came in lifting the cloak of misconception and invisibility from certain jobs and those who inhabit them.

> I never thought about certain jobs before. When I saw we were going to read about a bookbinder, it sounded so boring, but you now know it seems kind of interesting. (Tiffany T.)

> When I made a phone call this weekend, I couldn't help thinking about the operator. (Beverly)

I've been looking at the woman who works in the cafeteria lately. (Tamara)

Isn't this kind of consciousness-raising the deepest goal of education?

CHAPTER 9

Fences
Makes Bad Neighbors

For the past several weeks in sophomore English we have
been reading out loud *Fences*, by the Pulitzer Prize-winning
playwright August Wilson. My class set has eroded over the
years, and there aren't enough copies for every student, so I
can't assign reading at home. That's just as well, since in this
particular class half the kids wouldn't do the reading and
I'd be left to improvise a lesson capable of accommodating
the prepared and the unprepared alike. Besides, plays are intended to be seen and heard, and my students love to read
aloud.

"Okay, the scene we're reading today is just between Troy
and Rose, so does anyone want to read Rose?"

It's an uncertain market, selling these reading parts. Some
days when a mysterious vacuum has sucked all the oxygen
from my room, I have no takers. On other days it's as if the
kids are body-checking each other on their way to the front
of the cafeteria line. That's what it's like today. Trinette's and
Shonda's hands shoot up simultaneously.

"Why don't we try Shonda today?" I say, attempting to
project a measured tone of fairness.

"Uh-uh, Dr. Hoffman. You promised me I could do Rose today. Don't you remember—at the end of class yesterday?" Thus spoke Trinette.

Elaine backed her up. "She ain't lying. I heard you tell her that." Her words are a sudden squall that blows up out of nowhere to threaten our fragile little skiff.

Shonda's turn. "Them two little bitches always be lyin' to help each other out. I bet they mamas lied to their men about who was their real daddies."

Mama bashing can never be ignored. It's the grandmother of all provocations. "Your mama don't even get off her back long enough to fix your dinner."

"You ain't nothing but a great big old pussy," says Shonda, "and I'm a come over there and rearrange your face for you."

Now both girls are up out of their chairs. Shonda appears poised to vault the table and make good on her threat, while Elaine, caught in the crossfire between the two, is gathering up her books and her makeup-filled purse and is headed for the door.

"I'm getting out of here before we start fighting. I can't afford to be thrown out of school. My mama be all up in my face about it if I do."

Things are happening so fast, I'm standing flat-flooted while all this unfolds, capable of nothing more than gesticulating feebly in the girls' directions. Kathy, an undergraduate in a methods class at a local university, is visiting today, and I am embarrassed to say that my first thoughts are not for the safety of the girls and their classmates, but for how this drama is playing for Kathy.

"Elaine, please, as a special favor to me, just go back and sit down. I promise no one will hurt you. And Shonda, if you would can all the threats, I'd still like to have you read the part. Trinette, we'll switch in the middle so you can pick up and read Rose."

Attribute it to dumb luck on my part, but everyone backs off and they edge toward their seats.

The world is divided between those who think fast on their feet and those who don't. I place myself firmly among the latter. Even though I defused the *Fences* conflict for the moment, I was caught off guard by it and went home that day shaken by my failure to address any of the deeper issues of civility, violence, cooperation, and decision making that it raised. Last year's murder in the school was very much on my mind and, with no credit due me, I had managed to avoid violence this time.

Fortunately, teaching is more similar to baseball than it is to the Olympics. When you have a bad day in baseball, you're right back in the ballpark the next day with a chance to make adjustments. An Olympic flop may be forever.

It occurred to me that I could use our regular journal-writing time to reopen the issue in a context that would allow us to examine again what had happened. Our journal-writing routine, established from the very first week of the semester, calls for ten- to fifteen-minute journal-writing sessions on Monday and Friday of every week, followed by a voluntary trading of the day's entries with the class. I almost always write along with the students (a wonderful opportunity, by the way, to document the events in my classroom in an otherwise overbooked schedule) and take my turn reading my jottings when it seems appropriate.

On the day after the incident, I wrote:

I was pretty upset and shocked by the blowup between Elaine and Shonda yesterday. The anger and the insulting language exploded so fast that I wasn't expecting it; it's something that's never happened in my class before. I don't think everybody in my classroom has to love each other, but I do expect them to treat each other like human beings. I keep thinking about the murder in school last year and how stupid it was. And then there was the shooting in the high school in Brooklyn where two kids were killed for nothing. It seems like some people have so much anger inside that the first thing they think of is hurting someone else.

When I read my journal to the class, the students responded with their own reflections on the blowup. Many had also been shaken by the brush with violence. Several wondered what it all looked like to our visitor. "What must she think of us? Do you think she'll still want to be a teacher?" one student asked. In a lighter moment, another student said, "Man, her eyes got so big when they were arguing! She looked like she was expecting Shonda to pull a gun out of her purse and shoot Elaine right there." We were all able to laugh at this scenario, which hardly seemed implausible yesterday.

With the help of the journal, a bad situation had been transformed into an opportunity for honesty and a chance to explore ways to avoid similar scenes in the future. With the journal discussion as a backdrop, Elaine and Shonda both spoke with me individually about the incident, apologized for their behavior, and agreed to talk with each other about what had happened. There were no recurrences.

In all the many intriguing articles about journal writing and its value in the classroom, I had never come upon the idea of using it reflectively as a means of addressing issues that often go unaddressed for lack of a proper forum. In the journal, problems can be aired without preachiness and sermonizing, the kind of deadly package that loses students' attention. Although this should hardly be the primary purpose for journal writing, it's a side benefit worth capitalizing on. By turning the spotlight on situations within our common experience that troubled me or that are in need of a collective solution, I am modeling for the students an additional way for them to use their journals.

There were other occasions on which I had used the journal to bring to the surface festering problems and issues. Earlier this year I had arrived at a point of absolute frustration with the problem of undone homework. I wrote the following journal:

I'm wrestling right now with the question of homework for my regular class. The pattern is that I give an assignment that half the kids do. Then the lesson that I've built on the homework is a bust and I have to backtrack. The kids who *have* done the assignment get discouraged because we have to re-do the work in class. Then I have to give out a lot of zeroes and everybody starts feeling bad about themselves.

What are my choices? I can stop giving any assignments and do everything in class. Then we get very little work done because it would take almost the whole semester to read one book, for example. I don't like to lower my expectations because I know what it's going to take for the people here who want to go to college to be able to succeed. Even if they don't go to college, I want them to be educated and well informed. There are a lot of very intelligent people in this class and I want them to do well.

Are there problems interfering with schoolwork—like jobs? That's what I need to find out.

As soon as I was done reading, Monique led the chorus of respondents. She was squeezing two jobs into her day. Her routine involved heading straight from school to the day-care center where she worked as an aide and from there to McDonald's, where she and a number of her classmates put in more hours than on class time and homework combined. No wonder she was falling behind and nodding off in my class, although I knew her to be a diligent student, concerned about her grades to a degree that most of her peers were not. Rhonda's baby was sick a lot and she was spending a lot of time hauling her from clinic to clinic or waiting in line at the WIC office to make sure the baby was going to have enough food next month. Deion had two sisters and their babies living in the apartment with him and his mother, and the only way he could get any privacy was to climb into bed and pull the covers up over his head. This was not a posture conducive to studying.

Although there was an element of alibiing in these remarks, the problems were real and hearing about them gave me an appreciation of the obstacles we were all struggling against. The discussion even produced an ephemeral pickup in completed assignments, although the roots of the problem run too deep to succumb to any one-shot efforts.

Two more daring and problematic uses of the journal involved turning the spotlight on individual students who were causing problems for their classmates, for themselves, and for me, problems of a kind that did not yield easily to one-to-one encounters.

Sam arrived in my class in midsemester from a suburban high school where his teachers had seen his clinically diagnosed attention deficit disorder as plain old bad behavior and punished it accordingly. His parents were desperate for a more understanding environment for their intellectually gifted son. For the most part they found it in our school, although Sam's usually tolerant classmates did not take well to his unique blend of hyperactivity, immaturity, and arrogance. Sam drummed on the table, bounced in his chair, brought toy cars to roll back and forth on any available surface, and made wholly transparent claims about romantic encounters that were still years out of his reach. Students began to reinforce each other in aiming insults and sarcastic remarks at Sam, who attempted to conceal his hurt behind what he considered clever retorts.

Ignoring the situation could only lead to further deterioration, so I wrote about it in my journal and read the entry to

my class. I emphasized the need to arrive at a humane ac-
commodation that would enable us all to live out the semester together without inflicting any psychic damage. The class
was able to spell out for Sam all the aspects of his behavior
that irritated them while Sam testified tearfully to how tired
he was of being put down, laughed at, and abused by his
peers. Sam proved more capable of controlling his annoying
behavior than his clinical diagnosis suggested, and his classmates exercised admirable restraint in dealing with him for
the balance of the year. The operation was a success.

The final intervention-by-journal had a more enigmatic
outcome. Ben was a handsome young man with a Michael
Jackson hairstyle. Even in the Houston heat he often wore a
full-length leather jacket. His tastes ran to heavy gold rings
and neck pieces. Everything about Ben's presentation of himself was stamped "drug dealer" and the intermittent presence of his beeper was the cherry on the sundae. How to
deal with Ben's presence in the class? Should I report him to
the school's substance abuse monitor, hired by the school
district to deal with just such problems? If I accused him
wrongly, would I ever be able to work with him again? If I
failed to report him, what message was I conveying to the
other students in the class?

One journal-writing morning I laid out my dilemma,
along with all the incriminating evidence, in my entry and
read it to the class, with frequent glances in Ben's direction
to gauge his reaction, no easy task with someone schooled
in impassivity. He did seem vaguely amused, particularly
when his classmates began to berate me for my naïveté in
imagining that a real drug dealer would telegraph his identity so boldly. This was Ben's style, the kind of dramatic
statement he chose to make, nothing more. But what about
the beeper? It was his father's, Ben claimed, part of the professional equipment he used in his security business.

The discussion went most of the way toward convincing me that perhaps I was overreacting to Ben's trappings. I told him, however, that I would have to report the beeper, which was expressly forbidden by school rules. Our monitor, with a true flair for the dramatic, appeared in the middle of our class period the next day and asked Ben to accompany him to the office, where Ben repeated the same story about his father's security business. Next day he was back in class, as silent and enigmatic as ever, and I don't know to this day whether we had all been duped. Ben bore no grudges. Two years later he even stopped by to visit and let me know that he was working on getting into one of the local colleges. I don't know whether Ben was posturing again, but I do count it as some measure of success that he was talking to me at all.

In Ben's case, as in the others, the journal proved a constructive alternative to the silence that often encases classroom crises. How useful it would have been to have had a similar medium to help me through the missed chances and moments of bewilderment I experienced as parent and husband.

CHAPTER 10

Adam and Eve, Not Adam and Steve

Henry was a classic queen. He minced, he pranced, he pursed his lips when he spoke in class about his weekend filled with hairdressing gigs for various boyfriends. He was ecstatic when he was chosen as bandmaster for the school band, a position that allowed him to costume himself in a tall, plumed hat and brass-buttoned uniform and high-step before the appreciative football crowd.

Roderick radiated anger and barely contained violence when the subject of homosexuality came up in his class. When President Clinton had forced the issue of gays in the military onto the national agenda, Roderick unloaded in his journal entry about how much he hated fags, how if one of "them" ever touched him or put a move on him he would punch him out and stomp on him without any compunction.

When he disengaged from the issue of homosexuality, Roderick was a sensitive, thoughtful young man. The summer before he was in my class, Roderick had attended a camp run by a local interfaith organization and had returned with a newfound respect for other religions and for white people, with whom he had had little previous face-to-face experience. Yet gays, in their willful inclination toward sin and evil, were beyond the pale.

Roderick wasn't alone is his homophobia, which he claimed had been fueled by a gay man's attempt to get physical with his brother. Whenever the subject came up in class, someone was sure to trot out the clever slogan that could easily have been an ad agency creation: If God approved of homosexuality, He would have made Adam and Steve, not Adam and Eve. Roderick and his like-minded classmates, steeped in a combination of street macho and fundamentalist religion, were convinced that gays were doomed to go straight to hell, but they could repent and choose the right path because, after all, homosexuality involved a conscious choice, which could therefore be reversed.

Roderick and Henry were not in the same class, but there were less flamboyant Henrys in Roderick's class, invisible to their degraders and sometimes still unacknowledged even to themselves. They were doomed to turn on that spit of hatred almost daily, previewing the roasting that reportedly awaited them in the next life.

I never succeeded in damping Roderick's fury, but my failures with him and the vulnerable presence of Henry brought me to introduce Harvey Fierstein's *Torch Song Trilogy* into the play-reading unit in my Vanguard class one semester. In my regular class, *The Women of Brewster Place*, which includes a portrait of a lesbian relationship, drew generally unsympathetic responses; they drowned out the quieter chorus of "That's their own business" or "They ain't bothering nobody." I had not yet found the courage or the proper vehicle to confront the hostile attitudes head-on.

For readers unfamiliar with *Torch Song*, it is a pioneering theater piece—a pre-AIDS glimpse into the familial and love lives of gay men. Arnold, the central character, is a transparent stand-in for the author, who actually played the part in both the stage and film versions. He is by turns sharp-tongued, vulnerable, nurturing, and lovesick in his dealings with his mother, his lovers, and his adopted son. I hoped that students could see the universality of the themes: Arnold's quest for love, for acceptance by his family, for honesty in his relationships were what we all aspire to, regardless of sexual preference.

In addition to the way *Torch Song* deals with the emotional lives of its unusual characters, the play's success lies in its innovative structure. Entire scenes are built around dialogues between the on-stage characters and a mute off-stage partner. There is a fugue scene in which conversations between pairs of lovers in different rooms weave around each other like two melodic lines, at times harmonizing and at times producing cacophonous discords. It was the play's structural uniqueness that led me to think that the students in my creative writing elective might benefit from studying it.

I prepared the creative writing students by telling them that we were about to embark on some daring reading on a subject not often addressed in the classroom, and that the material might shock or upset them in places. I tried to focus on the structural aspects of the play, but I knew full well that these would quickly be subordinated to its characters and subject matter. I assured them that if anyone found the prospect of this reading troubling or thought their parents would have serious objections, I was prepared to make alternative assignments.

I have worked under supportive administrators who have never challenged my judgment in the selection of materials. My only previous brush with censorship had come in my small New Hampshire school when a parent complained about the presence in my class library of *Go Ask Alice*, a fictional journal of a teenage girl's descent into drugs and occasional prostitution. The superintendent was satisfied with my explanation of the educational value of the book; he expressed his support for me and the complaint died.

My supervisor knew about the *Torch Song* plans, but I did not bother to inform parents directly, as I usually would handle the use of controversial material. It seemed particularly pointless in a class where nearly half the students were already eighteen. Besides, my experience has been that if an atmosphere of trust and mutual respect exists between me and my students, they will find it in their interest to protect all of us from outside attacks in controversial situations. I also believe that there is no subject unapproachable in a classroom—or in a family, for that matter—provided it is open to honest discussion in a serious atmosphere.

I asked the students to keep reading journals as they worked their way through the play. The bulk of the entries were direct responses to the text—character analyses, expressions of confusion about the structure of several scenes, delight at the sheer entertainment the play offered:

> There is nothing better than a story with real humor. I know people were looking at me like I was crazy for the many times I laughed. I don't care. I like being educated with humor. The writers of my American Literature book should have lunch with Harvey Fierstein one day.

I was most interested in how the students reacted to reading about homosexuality and what changes, if any, the play wrought on their understanding of the world beyond school.

First, a small tribute to much-maligned parents who are often cast as villains in censorship stories, false protectors of their children's long-departed innocence. Imagine my relief on reading this entry by Karen, a vivid young woman whose family emigrated from El Salvador when she was seven:

One night, while I was reading, my mom walked into my room and asked me what I was reading. I mumbled the title! I didn't know how she was going to react on the topic I was reading about. The title didn't tell her much about the content of the book, so she asked me what it was about—I took a deep breath and told her that I was reading a play about gay guys. Well, I nearly fell off my bed with astonishment when my mother was approving the book and the teacher. She started telling me that the schools were afraid of teaching subjects of the "real world." Don't get me wrong, my mother and I are very open with each other, but I couldn't help but feel surprised. I guess it was because we had never touched the topic before.

Amy is a very demure, sensitive Asian-American student. Her entry reflected an even greater openness on the part of enlightened parents, who may represent the true silent majority in our schools. This brief glimpse of her mother shattered all my stereotypes of how homosexuality would be approached in that culture:

I went to Bangkok, Thailand two summers ago and my mother took me to see this drag-queen show called Alcatraz, and as I read this play, all those memories came flooding back to me. I could almost hear the music in the background and hear the drag queens doing their dancing/ singing routines. [In *Torch Song*, Arnold is a drag queen nightclub performer.]

What did the students think about the appropriateness of studying this play in school? Most did not address this issue directly, choosing instead to dismiss it by discussing *Torch Song* matter-of-factly, as they did all the other books they had responded to in their journals. But several responded head-on:

There are so many other things that public school students are exposed to. This book seemed to clear up some thoughts for me. It opens up the mind of a homosexual and a bisexual and allows you to peek inside and see beyond the title "gay."

I can't really identify with Arnold because I'm not gay, but I think that it is a great book. One that should be read by exactly this kind of audience. High school students are less likely to condemn the book because it is about gay people. I think adults are less open-minded about the subject of homosexuality. Adults should read this book, it might open up their thinking a bit.

Maria, a Hispanic-Catholic girl, was ambivalent and confused enough to articulate two seemingly contradictory views:

When I read this book I felt like I was doing something wrong because of the sex that was mentioned. I feel uncomfortable reading or seeing movies with this kind of activity.
BUT
I don't think there is anything wrong with studying this book in school. In fact, I think it's an excellent idea because [for]getting all the dirty stuff of the reading, we are allowed to examine how it is written. It even makes us think of homosexuality—that these two people actually love each other.

The one dissenting vote on reading this book at all came from Mark, a marvelously independent-minded young man who seemed to take issue with the reading on behalf of others:

The only thing that bugged me was the very sexual, graphic nature of the piece. It just didn't sit too well when I thought about this being done for a class. Our society is very sexual and shouldn't have to hide that fact, but there is a contingent that might be offended. I guess I would have picked another book, that's all, but it was good.

The journals were full of indications that reading the play had changed students' perceptions and attitudes. That's not the sole reason for studying literature, but it's certainly an important one.

Wow! I have never in my life read a book on the topic of homosexuality. Before reading the first page my attitude toward the topic had been blank. I was aware of homosexuals, but never thought about it or them.

I began to see that gay people are exactly like straight people. They love the one they're with, never mind that it is a person of their same sex.

I know plenty of people who have had the exact same experiences, except in a heterosexual situation . . . in identifying with Arnold, this story has helped me understand exactly how similar homosexuals are. I mean, I've never really thought they were like aliens or something, but I did kind of think there was something besides their sexual preference that made them different.

This play was really the one that made homosexuality seem not like just a bunch of sex, but of feelings and pain. I think it was the only one that dealt with the social problems of homosexuality, which is something I think has to be mentioned. Arnold summed it up for us when he says to his mother, ". . . try to imagine the world the other way around. Imagine that every movie, book, magazine, TV show, newspaper, commercial, billboard, told you that you should be homosexual. But you know that you're not and you know that for you this is right . . ." That scenario made me think about it and for the first time I began to really understand how awkward it would be.

By reading this book, I was exposed to a homosexual and I realized that they are people too. They think, feel and love.

Finally, this excerpt from Laura's journal in which the distance between school text and real life that sometimes seems unbridgeable is erased:

One of my best friends in the world is homosexual. He has some problems with the fact, inner and outer conflict with his gayness. It's not like having a friendship with a girl at all. Being R's best friend is the closest relationship I've ever had with anyone, including "boyfriends." R and I could talk about anything at all. He isn't as up front with his sexuality as Arnold, but they seem to have a lot of similar qualities. . . . I've always listened to and stood by R, but now that I've read this play, I feel like I can relate to him more since I've been through experiences similar to his in a symbolic sense of reading.

Why do we read except to live symbolically all the lives we will never live, to feel compassion for characters who, although they are not us, share with us a common humanity? The empathy reflected in these student journals and in the class discussions that sprang from them confirms the need to put aside our timidity and risk introducing unheard voices to our classes. I would like to imagine that even Roderick might have heard those voices and been moved by them.

CHAPTER 11

Tragic Endings

On a rainy midweek morning, I stood at the main office counter shedding water from my slicker as I initialed the sign-in space next to my name on the clipboard. Normally Alice, from behind her switchboard perch, would have twitted me about ruining her carpeting, but she was absorbed in an intense phone conversation.

"It usually would have gotten here twenty minutes ago, but it hasn't arrived."

Pause.

"Well, could you radio and see if it's broken down somewhere? If I don't have some information soon, I'm going to have to call parents. You know the way these parents are. They don't forgive me for not keeping them informed that their kid has sneezed today."

She hung up.

"What's happening, Alice?" I asked.

"One of the buses hasn't come in. Probably nothing."

By the end of the second period the bus carrying Vanguard students from distant parts of the city still had not arrived.

All morning rumors circulated through the school that the

missing bus had been in an accident; we waited for details. During my midmorning off period, Myron, the school psychologist, confirmed my worst fears. One student had been killed when an eighteen wheeler sideswiped the bus on a rain-slicked street. Several other students were seriously injured and had been transported by helicopter to Ben Taub Hospital in Houston's vast medical complex. Chellys, the dead girl, was in my English class. She was a vivacious, sensitive black girl who had caught my attention with her imaginative writing and a good ear for dialogue. Chellys was unique in her preoccupation with Dungeons and Dragons, a fantasy game that was usually the exclusive domain of the boys, who were drawn to its unique mix of power and magic. The interests she shared with the boys irked her clannish female classmates, who made her the butt of ridicule that had about it the unmistakable aroma of jealousy. Steve and John, two of Chellys's closest friends, classmates, and D&D partners, were among the most seriously injured.

How to break the news to the school? Sandy, our principal, wanted the kids to get the news in a way that cushioned the shock but allowed them to give vent to whatever emotions might be loosed by the tragedy.

We decided to call together the classmates of Chellys, Steve, and John and to be with them when the principal announced the bad news over the loudspeaker to the entire school. The students were accustomed to hearing Sandy's protesting a bit too much in her pure Texas drawl that she "love[s] and care[s] about each and every one of you." This happened to be true although it provided a ripe target for parody by students and staff alike. We had rejected the idea of dismissing school, sending the kids home to confront the tragic news away from what threatened to be the mass hysteria of several hundred students reinforcing each other's grief. It seemed better that we face death together, to draw whatever sustenance we could from the group and to have the students derive what meager wisdom they could from our professional counsel.

We pushed aside the chairs and tables in my classroom to make room for the three classes we had called together. From the carpeted floor we tilted our heads heavenward in the direction of the loudspeaker.

"Boys and girls, you know we love each and every one of you. We really do. But sometimes things happen we have no control over. At those times, we have to give each other a big hug to help us get through the hard times."

The kids, sensing the serious intent behind Sandy's words, restrained themselves from their usual pastime of parrying clever quips with the unctuous speaker voice.

"This morning there was an accident that involved one of our buses. Several students received minor injuries and were sent home after being treated at the scene. Three other students were transported to the hospital with more serious injuries which are not, thank the Lord, life-threatening."

It was clear now that Sandy had chosen to unfold the bad news in a fashion ghoulishly reminiscent of the announcement of contest winners, in reverse order of importance.

"And one student, poor Chellys Moore, died after being life-flighted to Ben Taub Hospital. They did everything they could to save her but did not succeed. I hope you'll all say a prayer for her in whatever fashion you see fit."

That blurred scene of the not yet lifeless body, wrapped in white, strapped to a gurney being wheeled onto a helicopter, blades still turning for the quick getaway, ran over and over like a recurring nightmare on the evening news. But the students, still on their bottoms on my carpeted classroom floor, were seeing that scene in their heads without the aid of media.

If there was more to Sandy's talk, no one heard it. After

a stunned silence, wails rose from various parts of the room, like distant sirens at the start of an air raid. Here and there, girls took Sandy's advice and fell into each other's arms in embraces of consolation. Students giggled reflectively, their emotional gyroscopes gone haywire. Others stared silently, unseeing, at fixed points, or as if in meditation.

We were together in that room for a long time, long enough for Rene to emerge from his prolonged trance to pound the wall with his bare fists, raging against the forces that had conspired to snuff out Chellys's life.

Amy, still seated, testified from her place, as if at a Quaker meeting.

"What gets me is that she'll never have a chance to fall in love, to go to her prom, to have children, to travel. It's not fair."

Myron and I tried to reassure the kids that all reactions were appropriate—tears, tearlessness, anger, silence, numbness. And we maintained this stance in the weeks and months to come, through the memorial service, the funeral, the return to school of the others injured in the accident. Some students wearied of what they saw as the excessive preoccupation with the accident in particular and death in general. Others never seemed to tire of turning the tragedy over in their heads, like a lump of coal, absorbing the light into its dark surface.

The ripples from the accident extended out over years. Two years later Rhea, one of Chellys's tormentors, revealed for the first time in her journals the burden of guilt she had carried in silence since Chellys's death; the accident had deprived her of the chance to make amends, to apologize for her childish cruelty.

For Steve, one of the students hospitalized after the crash, the reverberations have never ceased. For years after he graduated, he called me around the anniversary of the accident. Sometimes he was completely unconscious of the timing of his call. He was just feeling down and lonely. At other times, he was aware that he was seeking to exorcise the demons of the accident. Years later Steve called on the anniversary of his father's death after a long, painful struggle with cancer. The occasion unleashed torrents of emotion connected with his parents' divorce, his father's failure to fight for custody of him, the guilt his mother had invoked to get him to stay with her, the poignancy of his father's burial in a hillside cemetery where he had played as a child. Even here, the crash lurked in the background. As I urged Steve to get professional help to untangle the oppressive issues that had hobbled his academic career, he admitted that he held back from therapy for fear of what it might unearth about the crash that remained obscure behind an unbreachable shield and that he didn't care to remember.

A year later, the class suffered another loss. Jennifer, a close friend of a number of the kids who had been on the bus, had joined the marching band during her freshman year. On Thanksgiving morning the band gathered for practice before the afternoon's football game. Jennifer complained of a headache during the practice and within minutes was dead of an aneurysm in her brain. Some of her former middle school friends attended the memorial service in a funeral chapel on the edge of Houston's grim ship channel area, but an even larger number stayed away. It was as if they had spent themselves on Chellys's death and had no more to allocate to death from the meager resources of their fifteen-year-old lives.

By signaling to the students through our class readings and discussions that the deepest emotions and life dramas had a place in the classroom, I had laid the groundwork for the real-life confrontation with Chellys's death and with all the others. This one class's unique run of misfortune is reminiscent of Donald Barthelme's fiendishly brilliant short story "The School," which suggests a unique relationship between school and death. In it a teacher narrates an extraordinary chain of events, beginning with the death of the classroom plants, the class pets, a stray dog and a third world child the children adopt, some of the children themselves, and assorted parents and grandparents. Barthelme's deadpan recounting of these events wrings from us a life-affirming desire to laugh about the subject. It produced just that cathartic effect when it was read at a memorial service following Barthelme's own premature death from cancer. When I read this story to my students, its irreverent humor loosened tongues and opened the way for frank and painful discussions of death and loss.

Part of my reading program has always involved a component that allows students to choose their own books. In earlier grades, many of my students had read Katherine Paterson's *Bridge to Terabithia,* a powerful story about a childhood friendship interrupted by an accidental death. When I first read *Terabithia* out loud to a fifth grade class, I cried shamelessly at the heroine's death. My students were stunned by the intrusion of visible emotion into our classroom—and from a man, no less.

I like to believe that the reading and talking we had done about death in *Terabithia,* in *Tuck Everlasting,* Natalie Babbits's classic about a girl who rejects the offer of eternal life, in Judith Guest's *Ordinary People,* and in Fran Arrick's *Tunnel Vision,* where we see families dealing with the aftermaths of children's' deaths—that all these fictional encounters with death had prepared them in some small way for the real deaths that touched everyone in the group, and for the losses they suffered in their individual lives.

"Why are all the books you read in school so dark and gloomy? Isn't there something less bleak you can expose the kids to?" My challenger is a good friend, a former teacher, and a mother who has devoted herself to raising her three children well. She is a serious, hungry reader whose views cannot be dismissed as right-wing fulminations aimed at restricting kids' thinking and teachers' freedom. I've had my share of those worries, too. Maria's question arose from a deeper concern; she needed to understand whether school is shaping her kids into the kinds of people who would make her proud.

After playing back the reading lists of yesteryear in all the classrooms, grades five to twelve, that I have presided over in these past twenty years, I find myself guilty as charged. With very few exceptions, the books, both young adult and adult, that appeared on my reading lists have been a dark lot—tales of mental illness, suicide, racial hatred, religious prejudice, sexual abuse, divorce, and death.

But in spite of the depressing subject matter, the books are often uplifting testimonials to the power of the human spirit to survive adversity and even be ennobled by it. An encounter with social and religious prejudices leaves a character not crushed but strong, and clearer about who he or she is; a family wrestling with the suicide of a child is drawn closer by the bond of their common tragedy; a sexually abused child blossoms into a renowned writer.

We have to keep in mind Tolstoy's famous dictum that happy families are all alike; the stuff of serious literature has always been tragic, the anomalous, the "dysfunctional." Most vital fiction draws on the underside of human relationships and human emotions. The lives of the students who inhabit our classrooms are suffused with the same dark material that is the stuff of literature. In the past year, Maria's own three otherwise blessed children confronted within

141

their circle of family and friends alcoholism, mental illness, two instances of threatening cancer, physical abuse, and the progressive decline of aging grandparents. A teacher can tap any kid in the classroom and produce a gusher of a list that will parallel this one. Yet these tragedies and tragedies in the making find little reflection in what is addressed in school, where students and teachers act like parties to a pact to leave the "real" world outside where it will not disturb the orderly march through the bell schedule. When the subjects excluded from the agenda extend to poverty, racism, and social class privilege, the schools are engaging, consciously and unconsciously, in a process that Michelle Fine, in her study of high school dropouts, calls "silencing."

Younger children fare better than their older counterparts because in the traditional circle time and in the less fragmented familial elementary school classroom, there are structured and unstructured opportunities to talk about life on the outside. Most high school students have long since abandoned hope of finding links between school and the non-academic world. They may daydream or obsess over their worries when they should be taking notes or participating in class discussions, but beyond that, their real lives await them only at the other end of the school bus route.

Even when the books assigned in English classes offer openings to real-world anxieties and torments, students often find, to their dismay, that the material is approached as a set of artifacts outside themselves, to be perused, analyzed, dismembered, and—if they're lucky—reassembled. Rarely are they invited to explore how the books interact with their lives. Can Ophelia be a vehicle for thinking about what drives people to suicide, or is she the subject of an identification question on the next exam? Treating her as the former does not imply an abandonment of literature in favor of group therapy. It simply reconnects us with one of the basic impulses to find within a play some lessons for how to live their lives or how to make sense of what they have endured.

My friend Maria is too complex and thoughtful to be advocating a sweetness-and-light curriculum from which the darker side of human existence has been expunged. But there are others who would like to lay a heavier hand on the choices of what children may read and discuss. They need to recognize and respect students' hunger for honesty, for the penetration of real-life issues into the classroom. Young people are resilient. From their excursions to the underworld, they return armed to cope with what life has already thrust on them and what still lies ahead.

PART FOUR

Kids Center Stage

CHAPTER 12

Jeff:
The Miracle of Resiliency

Throwing chalk is a device mentioned in no extant manual of classroom management, but if you asked the kids in my class that year what they remembered most, they would tell you it was not *Othello*, not *A Separate Peace*, not the short story-writing project; it was the chalk.

There I am, pacing restlessly in front of the class, from stool to blackboard to my perch atop the back of a chair. When I turn from the board to face the class, there is Jeff buried in his book, seemingly oblivious to whatever inspired discourse I'm delivering. I've tried to ignore the fact that he has been thus absorbed since the beginning of class. It's not a statement of boredom or an act of defiance. Although it is early in the year, I know enough about Jeff already to guess that it is an act of self-protection, a futile attempt to wrap himself in a cloak of invisibility, a hope that this statement of disengagement will immunize him against the responsibility to perform. In fact, I suspect that Jeff is like the autistic children with whom I've worked. Without ever making eye contact or giving any hint of attending, they show evidence of absorbing everything around them, like giant satellite dishes pulling in signals from halfway around the globe.

Like the blooper-ball pitchers of my childhood, I loft the piece of chalk in Jeff's direction. To my delight and to the astonishment of the rest of the class, which is at least paying enough attention to take note of this bizarre act, the chalk's trajectory carries it through the narrow space between Jeff's nose and the open pages of his book. He looks up in astonishment. Adam leads the class cheer. "All right, Dr. H! What an arm! Nolan Ryan!" Always appreciative of acts of athletic prowess, Adam had been the organizer of the celebratory cake in honor of my two baskets in the Rogers faculty-student basketball game.

When Jeff looks up, I smile, compliment myself on my accuracy, which is, in truth, dumb luck, and welcome him back among us. He knows the chalk was not thrown in anger and there's good reason to assume from his later behavior that he saw it as it was intended, a reaching out to draw him back among us, a plea to put aside his shield in return for a guarantee of safe passage.

David, a student in one of my other classes that year, used his jacket in much the same way that Jeff used his book. He would never appear in class without it, and when the interior going got rough for whatever reason, invisible to the outside observer, he would pull the jacket up over his head and run the zipper right up under his chin until the smallest possible area of his face was left open and vulnerable to assault from the outside. Toward the end of the year we suddenly realized that David was showing up minus the jacket; he was informing us that he had passed into a new zone of safety.

I repeated the chalk-throwing gambit many times during the year, to the class's delight. It got to be a kind of game between me and Jeff in which I had the sense at times that he was burying himself in his book specifically in order to trigger it. There were even occasions when he roused himself in time to catch the chalk before it reached its mark.

Jeff was not at all aloof or unapproachable when I was alone with him. I had begun to invite him in from time to time to eat lunch with me in my classroom. Although the chalk throwing had created an important link between us, I needed to get beyond it. It was a lifeline I tossed to him, and he seemed willing to reach out for it. My invitation was spurred by a plea for help from Jeff's mother. She was a regular at our parent support group, which met every other Wednesday to discuss everything from achievement tests to shyness. Mrs. Randle was an attractive young woman who showed up at the meetings straight from late hours at work still wearing a business suit and ruffled silk blouse. She looked tired and harried.

Mrs. Randle rarely said anything during the meeting, but she always stayed behind to talk with me afterwards. She had divorced Jeff's father, remarried, and had another child. Like a number of his classmates, Jeff spent weekends and one month of the summer with his father. It was his mother's feeling that these visits with a demanding, rather emotionally inaccessible father were a source of great strain for Jeff, and were often followed by intensified bouts of the defensive reading Jeff did in class. Teachers had been complaining to her for years about his retreats, but no one had broken through them.

I needed to hear Jeff's version, which he was more than willing to provide. For several years we had run a discussion group at school for children from divorced families, and I learned from them in vivid detail how kids' needs fell to the bottom of their parents' agendas as they engaged in marital combat.

In fact, Jeff confirmed much of what his mother had repeated and added a few embellishments of his own. Jeff's father was a lawyer who had been heavily involved in left-wing politics. Some family friends whom Jeff knew well were currently in jail for their activities. Jeff knew more about politics than any sixth grader I have ever met. He could speak with great authority about Nicaragua and about American policy in Central America. When he did a paper and presentation on the subject in the seventh grade, his classmates were taken totally by surprise.

We met sporadically over Jeff's three years in middle school. As we nibbled absently at our sandwiches and apples in the stingy twenty-five-minute lunch periods, he would catch me up on the latest domestic battles. He was open, articulate, impishly funny. There was so much charm that he managed to keep concealed from his peers as well as from adults. We talked about the ups and downs in his academic work, which were connected to his problems at home, but not in any simple linear way. Although he was never anywhere near the brink of failure, he missed assignments or did them in haste, moments before they were due. The writing assignments he knocked off in the five minutes before class started were as good as pieces other kids had labored over at home.

Sometimes things really took hold and Jeff threw himself into a project with a full measure of passion. I remember a piece of historical fiction he wrote, a short story set during the revolution in China, a perfect synthesis of his reading, his deeply internalized family political values, and his considerable powers of imagination. Ironically, what was probably his best piece of work came at the most turbulent time of his life. I once interviewed a renowned Hungarian-émigré mathematician who told me he had reached his intellectual peak while he was fleeing from the Nazis, never sleeping in the same location two nights in a row. Jeff was fleeing his own demons.

One Friday night during his last year with me, Jeff's mother left him and his sister alone and told them she had some work do at the office. According to Jeff, this had been happening with increasing frequency and his suspicions were aroused. When it got really late and his mother hadn't returned, Jeff began to search around in her room, perhaps for some clue to her whereabouts. He found a packet that looked to him like cocaine and called his father for advice. Since my first meetings with his mother, the family balance had shifted and Jeff was now much more in his father's orbit.

He was at the age where he desperately needed that male force in his life. On his side, his father had softened and seemed less inclined to sit in judgment, readier to accept Jeff and appreciate his considerable gifts. At the same time, Mrs. Randle was becoming less accessible and more irresponsible. The cocaine was both cause and symptom of the changes in her life, which was spinning out of control.

Jeff's father called the police, who arrested the mother when she returned home late that night. Thus began a year-long battle in the courts, all too well publicized in Houston papers. The fascination of the case lay in the fact that Jeff and his sister had informed on their own parent. Mrs. Randle's defense attorney, one of the best in town, tried to build a case on the inadmissibility of evidence collected in this way. In spite of his efforts, she was convicted and the conviction was upheld on appeal.

Throughout all this Jeff and his sister continued to live at home with their mother. I imagine all three setting out together for court, where Jeff and Lisa would testify against their mother, and then returning home for the evening as if from an outing.

The strain on Jeff was enormous. Although his mother exercised admirable restraint in dealing with the children, she was at the same time making them pay emotionally for their act of betrayal. Yet Jeff was showing up in school every day, getting most of his work done, making pretty decent grades, and only occasionally playing hide-and-seek behind his book in class. He knew when my off periods were and would get a pass from his teacher, ostensibly to borrow a book from my class library, but also to snatch a few minutes to talk about the latest twists and turns at home or in court. Sometimes he just wanted to talk politics or books, a welcome respite from the press of his personal woes.

I remember coming upon Robert Coles's classic volumes, *Children of Crisis*. In the course of reading these extraordinary accounts of kids transcending the most difficult circumstances, I realized for the first time how primed I was to dwell on breakdown, defeat, malfunction. When we're looking at Jeff and thousands like him, it's far more impressive to consider the enormous strength and resilience that kids display under the most insufferable circumstances. There was Jeff, for example, hauling his suitcase and sleeping bag to the bus for our eighth grade overnight trip on the same day the mess of the trial, the conviction, and his role as informant were on public display in the local papers. He was determined to get on with his life, and he was succeeding with a dignity and courage that I would match against any act of battlefield bravery.

CHAPTER 13

Seth:
One-Man Underground

Everything about Seth seems oversize. If not for the unmistakable softness of his body he would look like one of those linebackers whose trunk-necked cameos decorate the announcements of the starting lineups for this week's televised Big Ten game. The tentative, curled position of his hands above the keyboard is not that of an athlete. Those hands lack confidence. As yet, they have not made peace with his body.

If you had never seen Seth erupt into one of his cyclonic rages, you might see him as a gentle giant, but here is take number ten of an oft-repeated scene. The hoarse, gravelly voice rises to an elephantine bellow, undeterred by attempts to calm or silence him, books slam down on tables, tables are overturned, and Seth storms out into the hallway, propelling the door so hard behind him that the posters on the bulletin board quiver.

Just as I began writing this piece I found a photograph of Seth I didn't remember owning. He is performing at a school banquet on his beloved keyboard, which rests atop a grand piano. Extension cords and wires snake around his feet, connecting him to the familiar collection of amplifiers, speakers, and microphones. There he stands, center photo, in characteristic posture—his left leg one step ahead of his right, his upper body tilted backward as if to exaggerate its already considerable girth. His shirt is creeping up out of his pants, gathered around the layers of fat that circle his mid-section. Wisps of long hair descend below the collar of the uncharacteristic white shirt he is wearing for this special oc-casion. The camera is a little too distant to reveal his pocked complexion, with its scattered acne eruptions, and one gets only a hint of how oversize his features appear up close.

Lithe spirits in fat bodies; nimble athletes trapped within crippled frames; self-conscious adolescents unaccountably enclosed in wrinkled, liver-spotted skins. So many of us are trapped in bodies we don't recognize as our own. They do not accurately represent to the world the image we possess of ourselves. I could never understand what impelled my eighty-five-year-old mother-in-law to refer to her friends as "the girls" until I realized that she did indeed see herself as a girl, forever looking over her shoulder for the old woman people seemed to be addressing when they met her.

Long before I met or taught Seth, his tantrums were leg-endary. His family belonged to our synagogue, and stories percolated up from the Hebrew school about this frighten-ing, oversize, out-of-control kid whom no one could reach. Later, when he graduated up into the synagogue's teenage youth group, in which my daughter was an active member, we were getting firsthand battle reports on Seth's tantrums, which disrupted conferences and dances. Peers and adults alike were irritated and frightened by his volatile behavior, which did not yield to any appeals for reason. That much fury in that big a body could do some real damage.

My first hint that there were other dimensions to Seth was at his Bar Mitzvah services in the synagogue. My wife and I came as part of our regular Friday night and Saturday morning routine, unaware that it was Seth's day in the spotlight. During much of the year there is a weekly procession of prepubescent boys barely tall enough to peer up over the lectern to chant their Torah portions, off-key, into the crook-necked microphone, and slightly more mature girls storming toward adolescence behind a cover of hairspray and eye makeup. And always the admiring, uncritical audience of family and classmates, a sea of heads adorned with skull-caps in the week's color scheme chosen by the family of the Bar or Bat Mitzvah child.

Seth's huge frame towered over the reading podium, and he proceeded to sing with clarity and feeling, every note positioned correctly. His Hebrew was as fluent and flawless as any Saturday performance I had heard. It was evident that there was a lot to Seth that was being obscured by the outbursts and by that message his body telegraphed to the world: Stay away from me. I'm scary and unpredictable.

I had had no firsthand contact with Seth, but I knew his mother from committee assignments we shared in the synagogue. Although she is a talented amateur artist, she was most known for two idiosyncratic qualities. First, without fail, she arrived at least thirty minutes late for any meeting or public function. For others this may have represented a fashionable conceit, but for Sandra it was a sign of the chaos reigning in her household, which explained so much of what I later got to see of Seth's style. From my one visit to their house, I remember piles of books and papers, unwashed kitchen utensils, and paraphernalia belonging to her uncommunicative psychiatrist husband, whose current career ran a distant second to his real ambition—to become a successful toy inventor.

Second, talking with Sandra was like standing under a shower whose spray had taken on a life independent of the faucet handles. No matter how you turned them, the water continued to pour down on you uninterrupted. Often after meetings, Sandra followed me out to the parking lot, not losing a beat in the flow of her monologue even as I unlocked the car door, slid in behind the wheel, fastened my seat belt, and started up the engine. It never occurred to her that it was time to break off until the car was actually in motion.

It was in the course of these monologues that I learned of Sandra's struggle to find a tolerable place for Seth within the labyrinth of the Houston school system. From his earliest years he had been "coded," a system of labeling children that stops just this side of taking a branding iron to them. The intent is humane: in order to be eligible for certain special services and individual attention, a student must be coded. But the label brings with it the inevitable stigma, and placement in "special education" classes often obscures the incredible range of differences among the students who are deemed "special." In Seth's case, it was somehow assumed that his severe emotional difficulties would be associated with equally severe learning problems. So many special ed kids were retarded or saddled with learning disabilities that it was assumed that all could benefit from the same tightly structured, work sheet-oriented kind of education.

It wasn't until late in Seth's middle school years that Sandra's campaign to convince his keepers that he needed something different paid off. His teachers began to recognize that Seth was far from slow. In fact, there were hints of brilliance. Here is Seth's own account of that moment of redefinition. It comes from a surrealistic story he wrote in my class in his senior year of high school that began as a kind of exposé of the treatment of SPEDS (as he called special ed kids) by one of the rare survivors of that near-death experience who returned to tell the tale.

He's working too fast said my overseer, the one in the
white coat. I hadn't noticed said an older man.

—Can't you see he's done fourteen problems in the last
minute

—Doesn't sound too bad to me after all it's only squar-
ing and square roots

—But look how long it's taken the others I suspect
something

—What are you thinking

There's a pause over seven years of education.

—It might be mislabeling

—How do you get that

—Why else would it be so easy for him

—Look he's been tested four times and sent back every
time

—What did the tests say

The older overseer extracts a file from a recess of the white
coat. He reads.

—Says it right here definite behavioral disorder originally thought it was autism

—But if it's behavioral then why's he working on this stuff

—Standard curriculum

—But he's obviously

—Look I don't want to be argumentative but we can't
make exceptions

—He hasn't blown in a long time his temper is well
under control he's been on level three for two months

—What are you suggesting

—Maybe we should try him outside

—Don't be ridiculous

An overseer in jeans joins the conversation.

—Outside ready cases are very rare

The three remaining overseers stand in the background.

—Why not

—We'll consider it I'll have testing look again

—To hell with testing just look at him

Sandra had found a place for Seth in the city's high school
for gifted students, a place where in fact not everyone is

gifted, but where many of the kids are "different" in ways
that made their adolescent years a living hell but would
serve them well in their adult lives. It was the beautiful gift
outfit you had to wait to grow into. This new school world
was a liberation for Seth, and the first taste of it reinforced
his anger over the years of misguided constriction and bleak-
ness in which he had been forced to dwell.

> So this is what lies beyond I thought. I had heard that there
> was life outside the steel cubicles of the room where the
> misfits are thrown. The overseers certainly made sure that
> it wasn't seen, probably because it was so hard to under-
> stand or bring order from, and it was their duty by oath to
> keep the speds' pursuit simple.

At the end of Seth's freshman year I was transferred to
his high school, and there on the first day of school I found
him in my sophomore English class, his considerable presence parked within arm's reach of me at the front table from
which I operated, a place that students tended to avoid. The
more distance you put between you and the teacher, the
greater control of your participation in the proceedings you
retained. If a wide moat separates you from the teacher, you
are free to "veg out" when the inner voices call.

For Seth there was great security in proximity to the
teacher. The dangers, real and imagined, lay among his
classmates. In fact, in this community of deviants Seth was
not mocked or rejected openly by his classmates as he might
have been in the conventional Friday-night-football suburban high school where the parking lot overflows with BMWs
and Suzuki Samurais. He was like an extraterrestrial, un-
schooled in the etiquette of teenage social interaction, unable to decode the secret language of social appropriateness.

Seth entered the room laden with backpack, boom box,

and an armful of loose books and papers that he proceeded to broadcast around a wide radius from his seat—crumpled loose-leaf sheets containing assignments of indeterminate origins, binders with pages only half attached, paperback books almost stripped of their cardboard covers. And the search for that day's assignment, which had almost always been done but could almost never be found, would cause Seth to go ballistic, as the kids would say. First the low patter of self-denigrating comments, building quickly to a crescendo of self-flagellation. "Of course I can never find my work, but everyone in class has theirs. I am so stupid that I can't seem to follow the simplest directions. I don't know how any one person can be so stupid. I don't know what's going to become of me. I don't deserve to be here."

Once, Seth decided he was going to create a science fiction opera for which he would produce both the music and the lyrics. When he submitted to me the poems that were to be the core of the opera's opening numbers, I followed my usual practice of suggesting deletions, word changes, reorganizations—all in a day's revision work. Seth grunted. His hands began to flap, poised to do himself harm.

"I knew it. They're no good. I might as well throw them away."

"But, Seth, no writer gets things perfect the first time around. Revision is just part of the process."

"Oh, you can say that but look at how much is wrong. By the time I make the changes, there won't be anything left of the original because none of it was any good in the first place. How is it that other people can write stuff that turns out okay? I must be the stupidest person in this class."

For anyone else this self-condemning tirade might have been a backhanded appeal for praise, but for Seth it was dead-serious business. He allowed himself little margin in

159

his quest for perfection, and as a result his performance could never approach the standards he had set. Any shortfall tripped the air raid sirens.

Most of the students had learned to avert their eyes during these outbursts; they pretended to busy themselves with other things. They knew what was coming and in spite of knowing that the only casualty of Seth's fury was Seth himself, they feared that they might be swept into the path of his monsoon inadvertently and suffer unintended harm. A few students called out words of encouragement, reassuring Seth that the missing paper and the minor mistake were no big deal. I did my best imitation of the eye of the hurricane, neither indulging nor condemning the outbursts, simply plunging deeper into the lesson and when it looked like things were about to blow, suggesting to Seth that he take off for the hall or the counselor's office, where he could erupt in relative peace. Later, as Seth improved, he refined his own early-warning system and didn't need an invitation to take off *before* the storm hit.

During the dead time before his bus arrived, Seth would reappear in my room at the end of the day in as close to a state of composure as he ever achieved, eager to analyze his latest explosion and to wonder at what his classmates would think of him now. In a pattern that persists to this day and that echoes his mother's parking lot decorum, Seth would follow me around the room as I erased the boards, unplugged the coffee pot, gathered up piles of assignments to be carted home for grading. He would hold forth without any expectation of response from me and seemingly without even the need for any evidence that I was attending to him. Yet I knew from my work with autistic children that the apparent obliviousness to human interaction often masked a radar-like acuteness to all the nuances of people's responses to them. Seth was certainly not autistic, although he had been misdiagnosed as such early on, but I suspect that he shared some of that same camouflaged hyperawareness of others' responses to him. Out of the corner of my eye I would watch his hands working awkwardly, always one beat ahead of his speech, like perched house birds exercising their wings in anticipation of a never-consummated flight.

One day in the second half of that sophomore year Seth showed up in school with a heavily bandaged hand. In a rage with himself over some imagined shortcoming, Seth had pounded a glass door. His hand went through the glass, and the resulting cuts required a number of stitches. Judging from his reaction, it was probably the most therapeutic event in his life, next to his liberation from special ed. Somehow it scared Seth into an awareness of how really dangerous and frightening his explosions were. The real damage he had done to himself had simultaneously awakened him to what his behavior looked like to others and left him despairing about how he could ever possibly erase the perceptions people had of this raging grizzly, this tormented soul unaccountably trapped in a bear suit. Would there ever be redemption from past sins not even of his own making?

Slowly, the tantrums subsided. During Seth's junior year he was not in any of my classes but I tracked his progress through his English teacher, who had adopted the same style of low-key benign neglect of Seth's occasional liftoffs, combined with abundant praise for his unique and considerable gifts.

In his senior year he was back with me, fresh from a summer of jazz workshops and general unwinding. For the first time he had not gone off to the summer camp where his earlier reputation meant placement with the "weird" kids in a unit separate from the main camp. The positive aspects of the camp situation were overshadowed by the damage to Seth's ego caused by this carryover from his previous life in special ed. I anticipated a really stressful year as college choice and leaving home approached, but invisible tectonic plates were in motion, sliding and shifting into configurations bound to create new, unimagined continents.

Every classroom is a miniature religious denomination. Its rituals and traditions are soothingly predictable, but in rare moments they provide a springboard for those odd epiphanies that justify the whole enterprise. In my classroom, journal-writing time on Monday and Friday mornings was as unmistakable a ritual as morning mass. As we wrote, background music accompanied us—jazz, blues, classical, soul. The music set a mood and drowned out the distractions of slamming lockers, hallway chatter, and passing cars. And after the allotted ten or fifteen minutes the congregants were invited to testify by reading what they had produced that day. There was never any obligation to read, because the journals were private documents that I never inspected, unless I was invited to. On most days, I wouldn't have dreamed of exposing my musings to public scrutiny.

But Seth was heroic in these public moments. At the ritual call for readers, Seth's hand would rise timidly as he looked around to see if he was going to be all alone. The class always squirmed uncomfortably as Seth began, because what might emerge that day was unpredictable. Sometimes it was an artistic or verbal experiment. Seth had evolved a technique for making the background music the centerpiece of his writing, spinning out imagery suggested by the music. The results were often brilliant. His verbal facility was increasing at a breathtaking rate. He distilled stylistic lessons from everything he read: Kafka, Hesse, Kerouac, Barthelme, Calvino—a predictable list for a precocious adolescent. The class admired these pyrotechnics although they didn't fully understand them, and Seth's experiments encouraged a wave of imitations. What greater compliment? Seth was acquiring a reputation as a Writer, no small accomplishment in this little community of highly competent writers.

Then there were the days when Seth read an intimate entry in a soft voice that carried over the uncomfortable silence. He wrote about his loneliness, his fears that people might be stuck forever with their perceptions of the old Seth while he was evolving and growing into someone else. Always the central image was one of birth—not rebirth but *birth*. The self that had inhabited the special ed world was mechanical, nonhuman. "And some are born without pasts," went the opening line of one of Seth's stories. Seth's early years, devoid as they were of human relationships, left him with no history and few clues about how to comport himself with others. In a letter that was too intimate to read to the class, he professed his love for a classmate, an engaging and thoughtful young woman:

> What does a desperate, lonely, Hesse and Kerouac-addicted jazz musician type do? Yell out love to the world? Hold emotional forces back by concealing it with the force of emptiness? . . . What with living such a sheltered life as mine I almost feel as if I wouldn't know what to do going out with *anyone*.

Seth was coming awake inside a strange body, surrounded by an incomprehensible world. In a period of months he was being forced to synthesize social lessons others had absorbed over a lifetime. His reading and writing provided some valuable supports for the emergence of Seth's butterfly from its gray and brittle cocoon. The writing gave voice to the stirrings of feelings and self-awareness. The reading provided a set of conceits and devices that helped capture the flavor of the absurd world from which he was emerging and the often unapproachable world he was now attempting to inhabit. But as with a lot of his most clever contemporaries, the absurdist, nihilist, surrealist material he found so appealing sometimes created new obstacles in his journey to find himself. The intellectual cleverness obscured real feeling. The extraordinary pyrotechnics of Seth's writing sometimes made it impenetrable, and Seth wanted above all to communicate—to understand and to be understood.

Here is a note Seth left for me close to the end of his senior year:

> I think I've lost my last cover. I don't know where to go now. Are my surrealism and deep sensualism and my absurdism all as [much] a part of me as I thought. I don't want to be nihilistic . . . but I want my writing to be honest and pure and understandable. [Yet] I still want color and complexity like jazz. Where can I go?

At the same time Seth was demonstrating an understanding of the connections between literary style and the state of the writer's soul, and using the writing concerns as a metaphor for how he wanted to live his life. It was the final labor pain in Seth's birth process.

In the last months there were other auguries of good things to come. The college application process was as fraught with anxiety as I had anticipated. There were misplaced letters of recommendation, late essays, strained encounters with his mother over deadlines. Yet somehow it all got done, and Seth even managed to go off to Florida on his own for a campus visit, a feat I never would have imagined him capable of just months earlier. What had they made of him, I wondered, this boy-man with the odd mannerisms, the somewhat overwrought style of speech, and the unevenly calibrated social antenna. Weird or exotic? The difference is only a matter of semantics.

The acceptances came rolling in, though not always with

the necessary financial support. But one school in a large Southern city, impressed by his SAT scores and his astronomic grade point average, courted him with a full scholarship offer—pure balm for a bruised ego. The school was Catholic, an amazing irony for this committed Jew who had taken to wearing a skullcap to school and who had adopted as a personal logo a Jewish star with an infinity sign at the center and a hand reaching up from below as if to grasp it. It is a sign of Seth's newfound strength that the religious issue did not deter him from accepting the school's offer, but it also promises to secure his role as an outsider for a while longer.

New Year's Eve and prom night are emotional minefields for socially conscious teenagers. Can you find an acceptable date? Should you be participating in the first place? If you choose not to go, will everyone see it as sour grapes? If you do go, can it ever be anything but a disappointment after all the expectations you've built up? Seth, who did not figure to be a player in this particular dating game, surprised everyone. On one of our last journal days he read with a historic flourish:

> Rumors have been hovering over Jones Vanguard like vultures that Seth Barry Miller has evolved some form of a life. This runs contrary to all current theories backed up by the most prominent Sethologists and Get-A-Lifologists. . . . Particularly interesting are the speculations that Mr. Miller has not only evolved a life, but has involved a female in this life and that he and she will be present at the prom in the context of a relationship. The paradox . . . herein is that Seth Barry Miller as the single member of the one-man underground has probably taken no dating vows within himself, partly dismissing dating as a shallow bourgeois institution, partly seeing himself as mortally inferior to all alternatives and intelligent females.
> But let us cut to the chase, shall we? The question . . . is

this: Does Seth Miller, in fact, date and does he intend to carry this dating to the prom?

We will tease the reader with a smidgen of tasty suspense here.

And go he did, with a young lady who had scrawled her phone number on a cereal box top for Seth at a dance sponsored by his youth group. He knew she was not the love of his life, but she was a girl and she was in hot pursuit. That was a first. Seth dreaded the prospect of seeing his unacknowledged true love at the prom with her very real boyfriend, and the evening held endless possibilities for disaster. On Monday morning, I asked hesitantly how things had gone. Seth reported that he had made a wrong turn on the way home and had wandered through unfamiliar territory in the industrial area around the ship channel. No disaster, not even a word of self-condemnation for making a driving mistake. Just a normal kid on a normal Saturday-night date.

Immediately after school is out every year, Seth's youth group holds a big regional convention. At this event each of the seniors bids farewell to the group in a brief valedictory address. The same Seth whose presence had annoyed and frightened the others in earlier years moved the audience as he spoke of how lonely and isolated he had been in the organization. He cast no blame, but simply acknowledged that he had not been ready to engage with them, did not know how to reach out to the hands that had been proffered. But now he was ready—witness his ability to stand before them to make these remarks; *he* was reaching out to *them*.

The one-man underground was surfacing, leaving behind his darkest, most cumbersome, Dostoyevskian cloak, wearing instead the lighter, looser-fitting garment in which his alien, oversize body could dance to the music he creates.

CHAPTER 14

Deborah:
Backing Up for the Long Jump

This year I was ready. The "writing workshop," which had already become a fixture elsewhere, was to be the structure of choice in my English class at long last. Students would select their topics and genres and work at their own pace. Of course, through minilessons I would guide them to new techniques and forms, but basically the lockstep days were over—no more universal assignment due on the same date for all students.

Not all kids line the parade route to cheer the liberators. Being cut loose from the safety of teacher-prescribed work is like living away from home for the first time: there are meals to cook and laundry that needs doing. You pay a price for independence, and some would rather keep their semi-apartment in the family basement, meals included. Other students are doubtful about the sincerity of the invitation to take charge of their own writing. This is school, after all, and the good faith of the authorities is forever in question. Yes, there is student government, but when has it made a decision not condoned by the principal? And when has the literary magazine ever been free of adult screening? And how often has a student had his wrist slapped for advocating an unorthodox position in a class discussion that had been advertised as "open"?

The first exploratory probe of the newly announced writing freedom came almost immediately. Deborah asked to see me after class. Although she was a senior, I knew nothing about her because she had just transferred in at the beginning of the year from a small town outside of Houston. Deborah's round cherubic face, padded with traces of baby fat, had an air of innocence about it. Her bowed mouth was carefully painted with a deep shade of lipstick, and she wore scholarly rimless glasses. She dressed neatly, almost primly, and, unlike her classmates, almost never wore pants. In her nonstop smile one could read an extraordinarily complex mixture of innocence and flirtatiousness.

Deborah was concerned about the freedom to choose her writing material because there was in fact only one thing she was interested in writing about—Jesus. She had brought along a prose piece about her involvement with a Pentecostal church that had helped her find a new life through Christ. "In my old school, when I talked about my church and Jesus, people got upset. They said that kind of talk didn't belong in school and that I was preaching at them." Deborah was not the kind who enjoyed conflict and confrontation. She was offering me a face-saving way out of my blanket invitation to freedom. All I had to say was, "Well, Deborah, religion is another matter. Separation of church and state, and all that." She knew I was Jewish, as was one of her best friends in the class, and she didn't want to offend us. Wasn't it best just to bury the subject?

I didn't expect my test by fire to come so quickly. A lot was riding on my response. I told her that my job was not to prescribe what was legitimate for her to care about, nor to censor her thoughts. Instead, my task was to help make her writing—on whatever subject she chose—the best it could possibly be. I would deal with the writing as writing, not as polemic, and help her aim for clarity, good organization, richness and freshness of language, regardless of whether I agreed with her ideas or not.

As I delivered these high-minded pronouncements I wondered how well I could abide by them. I had been tested once by a student piece that had racist overtones. Although I was able to grade it objectively and make revision suggestions, I also unloaded on the ideas and expressed my dismay that someone in what I considered a successfully integrated classroom could harbor such prejudices. My comments did not open a dialogue between us. Instead it had a chilling effect. Kyoki never raised the issue again and I was left to question the wisdom of my response. As a strongly committed Jew I had reason to worry about whether I was up to the challenge of a Pentecostal Jesus.

The following week, Deborah turned in a poem, her first completed piece since our discussion.

Now in God's Hands

Obey thy parents
Is what the Bible commands
And I have tried so hard
To follow their every demand.

But something went wrong.
It happened along the way
And even though I was so hurt
I still tried to be good and obey.

Finally things piled too high
For me to understand.
So I turned to God's son—Jesus
And asked for a helping hand.

Now Jesus is my Savior
I talk to him when I pray

And I am really trying
To follow the Lord's saving way.

So at last I'm in line
And glad to be in God's hands
Now marching in the Lord's army
Ready when the trumpet demands.

I read on, filled with a strange sense of relief. Here was a poem like so many other high school creations, sincere in intention but riddled with weaknesses of language that could be addressed independent of its subject matter. My prejudices against the abcb greeting-card rhyme scheme (so subtly deployed in the best of hymns) were going to be more difficult to overcome than the promotion of Christian salvation. I could point out to Deborah the opportunities she lost when she used vague words like *something* and *things;* the places where specific details would result in livelier language and more interesting reading—what were her parents' demands, how was she hurt, just what is the Lord's saving way?—and the glaring clichés, like "helping hand" and "marching in the Lord's army," that needed to be expunged.

As I had promised Deborah with a confidence that belied my own doubts at the time, it did seem possible to put aside differences in philosophy and belief and look at a piece of writing as material in need of revision, just as if it were about baseball or wildflowers or childhood memories. I don't know how far I care to push the issue of whether any content is amenable to the same treatment. A budding Dr. Goebbels would hear from me about more than the use of cliché and the need for detail. But religious belief is private, of no direct harm to anyone else. And the Bible is filled with great religious poetry, so there is nothing inherent in the subject matter that precludes good writing. If there is a grand tradition of the poetry of bigotry and viciousness, I am unaware of it.

Deborah was relieved too. My responses seemed to convince her that I was a man of my word. She revised her poem in the same businesslike spirit in which my suggestions had been offered. I wish I could wow you with the finished product, which Deborah and I both agreed was an improvement over the original, but it is lost in the avalanche of papers that engulfs every English teacher and threatens suffocation over the course of a trying year.

But what evolved from this point with Deborah was as wondrously unpredictable as the writing process itself. The links between starting point and ultimate destination remain dimly discernible even as they grow increasingly more obscure. It will surprise no one to know that Deborah's writing extended far beyond her originally announced religious boundaries. Her deeply felt love of the church had roots in a tangled and troubled personal history, but she needed time and trust before addressing that in writing. I felt as if the religious pieces were lofted as trial balloons to gauge my trustworthiness as accepting audience.

Every Thursday lunch hour my classroom undergoes a personality change. Half a dozen seniors appear with the politically incorrect array of cupcakes, candy bars, and canned sodas they call lunch and move the chairs into a tight circle. This is Senior Support Group, a place to unload some of the considerable burdens kids bear in their final year of high school, the time—they will tell you with unveiled sarcasm—that is supposed to be the best of their lives. The talk is of pressures from college applications, concerns about leaving home, parental irrationality, thwarted romances, overdemanding teachers, infuriating siblings, betrayed friendships. The atmosphere careens between high seriousness and out-of-control tension-breaking silliness, all of it characterized by a sense of trust. Guard is down during this pathetically brief hour because the people in the circle have abided by the compact upon which the group is founded: nothing that is said in the group goes beyond these four walls. Sometime midyear, Deborah began coming to the support group sessions. One of her best friends was a main-stay of the group and convinced her to give it a try. She sat through the early sessions with a plastered-on smile that did little to conceal her discomfort over the proceedings. She had one toe in the water and still hadn't decided whether it was too hot to warrant a further step. Startling admissions and revelations lit up the air like flares over a battlefield—alcoholic boyfriends, parents in dire economic straits, long-concealed crushes (these from Seth, up from his underground lair for a weekly gulp of human air).

Through it all Deborah remained silent. The members of the group performed like skilled clinicians in allowing Deborah her silence. They never demanded reciprocal reve-lation. This was not a game of Truth or Dare in which she felt challenged to remove her shirt because the others were already bare-chested. There was the sense that whatever needed to would emerge in its own good time. Nonetheless I'm sure I was not alone in my curiosity about just what Deborah's story was. All I knew was that she did not live with her parents. Period.

Several months later, Deborah appeared with a piece of writing very different from her earlier religious poem. She explained that her college applications had grown more and more burdensome, because she was unable to provide the schools with what seemed like routine information about family finances. It appeared best to use our open writing contract to produce a letter of explanation for the colleges, for me, and for her fellow group members, and it parted the curtain on some of Deborah's story. When she handed it to me, it was neatly typed and photocopied, a document that looked official, for the record, like a court deposition.

> This letter has one basic purpose, to help you understand my background a little better to enable you to answer questions that I have. It is very possible that on both the admission and financial aid applications I am submitting to your college or university, that you will find several questions unanswered. Most likely they will deal with my parents or something of that nature. At this time I would like to explain the circumstances surrounding my background and then maybe you will understand why there are questions that remain unanswered.
>
> I do not currently live with my parents. My real father and mother were divorced when I was two. My mother remarried, and I was adopted by Mr. B**** at the age of six or seven. They later divorced. She married her current husband in, I believe, 1985.
>
> I ceased to live with my mother and second stepfather on Thursday, May 4, 1989. On this particular date, I was removed from school by a local highway patrol officer and taken home. The reason was that my mother and stepfather were being arrested by the F.B.I. (To this day, I still do not know the exact charges that were brought against them.) I have two younger brothers, and two younger sisters. The oldest boy and girl were both in junior high at the time. I had to go home and take care of the youngest boy (now 3) and the youngest girl (now 4½). Once the F.B.I left, we were taken to a Justice of the Peace's office until the lady from Children's Protective Services could come.
>
> From May 4, 1989, through the present, my mother has not helped support me in any way. It is virtually impossible for me to get my mother to consent to fill out any type of papers for me. This leads to problems with many of my admissions applications and financial aid forms. None of the families with whom I have resided can legally fill the forms out, since I was not placed in any of their care by a court order—when I was sixteen, it was with my grandparents' permission; once I turned seventeen, it was on my say-so.

The body of the letter consisted of a long, heartbreaking account of Deborah's peregrinations from home to home as she was taken in for short periods by an assortment of grandparents, pastors, church friends. Some had been grudging hosts, others nothing short of saintly in the way they had opened their homes to her. The letter left me near tears for all that was left unsaid about the emotional toll these wanderings had taken—two years with patches of love from relatives and friends but no consistent source Deborah could look to for support or advice. She had gotten herself into our special high school on her own and her journey to college would require similar self-propulsion. Behind that permanent Kewpie-doll smile lay a world of strain. Deborah was a beautiful ceramic vessel at risk of cracking when the kiln temperatures were turned up.

In the last months of her senior year, those stress lines grew more visible. The pressures of college application multiplied as Deborah faced the question of how far from the safe haven of her church she was prepared to wander. To complicate matters further, without any steady source of adult advice she had failed to take the SAT exams at the proper time, and some of the schools that were interested in her were handcuffed by more than the lack of parental signatures on the financial aid forms.

Although Deborah had developed very methodical work and study habits that included maintaining detailed lists and calendars of assignments, she was drowning. "I try, I really try to keep up with the work, but sometimes when I sit down with it there's so much to do until I don't know where to begin. My teachers act like I'm supposed to know all this already, but I don't. Maybe it wasn't so smart for me to come down here in the first place."

Her small-town high school background had left her ill-prepared for our school's high-powered academic program.

To her teachers in the advanced placement courses she seemed more and more out of place among her fast-moving classmates. She had laid out an extremely ambitious independent study reading course with me and fell farther and farther behind. Together we adjusted and readjusted the workload until it seemed manageable, but her body was joining her psyche in its rebellion against the pressures of the past two years: she was getting sick and missing school with a regularity that was a reminder of the wisdom of heeding the delicately calibrated alarm system we carry within us.

Her church life sustained Deborah through this down time, but she had also come to realize that writing offered the possibility of some relief as well. Did I think, she asked, that writing her life story could help her feel better? That was like the chickens asking the fox if he might not be hungry. Even posing the question was a validation of the stance toward writing that I had taken with Deborah and her classmates. During the last week before finals, Deborah brought me daily a new installment of her life story and stopped in briefly at three-fifteen, before the bus arrived, to elaborate on what was in the written text. I suppose that the approaching end of school, and with it our relationship, made for a relatively safe form of revelation, but there was no search for safety in what she wrote. It was a tale of an immature and impressionable mother falling into ill-advised marriages, one of them to a man who abused Deborah. Rather than protecting her from the abuser, her mother doubted her daughter's veracity and eventually accused her of breaking up her marriage. Only a totally trusting and supportive grandmother pulled the wounded child through.

Finals week brought the autobiography to an abrupt end. But the crucial, difficult chapters had been written and with them Deborah had taken some enormous steps in understanding herself, in allowing others in as partners in that understanding, and in recognizing the powerful role that writing can play in asserting control over a life in danger of throwing its tentatively perched rider. Deborah graduated but didn't make it to college the following year. She needed time to consolidate her gains, which she did within the safe confines of a supportive, albeit somewhat stifling, surrogate family. She's living independently now, successfully moving up through the ranks of a small communications firm in another state. It won't be long before she's ready to continue her education. In our year together, Deborah and I had both risked ourselves. Together we had backed up a considerable distance from that long-jump line and, to our surprise, found ourselves instead in an entirely different event, gliding gracefully over the impossible reaches of the finely balanced pole-vault bar, surveying the pitted terrain from a revealing height.

CHAPTER 15

Melanie:
Stolen Moments

Melanie and I arrived at Jones High School at the same time, I a willing immigrant from my middle school job, she an exile, forced out of the performing arts magnet high school (PVA) when they dropped instruction in a number of instruments, including her beloved harp. For Melanie it was an expulsion from Eden, and she was not willing to forgive Jones for being a second suitor for her affections. PVA had finally seemed like home after a childhood of strangeness and alienation. Serious eye problems required a series of operations and long stretches out of school. It was the perfect crucible for the formation of an introspective, artistic, fantasy-rich self, the experience of being forced back early on one's own resources that appears so often in the biographies of writers and artists.

The only remaining physical legacy of that dark time were the thick glasses that guarded her wide eyes. Melanie wore no makeup and on most days dressed in black, in the best PIB tradition. (That's a Person in Black, or so my students—taking pity on their unhip old teacher—informed me.) But there was always an extra little flourish, an affirmative statement beyond the basic black. Sometimes it was a little wreath of flowers she wore like a halo. Once while we were studying Hawthorne's "The Minister's Black Veil" she came to class with a black shroud draped over her indifferently tended hair. Through the entire lesson she sat unspeaking, an eerie but effective embodiment of the story's essence. Sometimes the embellishment was a subtraction; whenever she could get away with it her feet were bare, in clear violation of school rules. Another teacher, disdainful of the figure Melanie cut, called her a hippie. There was a lot more to her than could be encompassed in that label, but she certainly paid homage to her cultural and stylistic ancestors.

The terms of my relationship with Melanie call for a new label—graphotherapy, perhaps. Melanie was one of the most prolific writers I've known. In the time it took others to complete a one-page entry in their journals, she did five. A note of explanation accompanying an assignment became an essay in its own right. Although students can choose to keep their journals as private as they like in my class, Melanie often slid hers over to me as she completed them, beginning a cycle of correspondence that soon became voluminous. There were letters left on my desk at the end of the day, notes attached to assignments, poems, and stories for my comment. In those early days when she was a student in my sophomore English class, we actually spoke little. Although that was no longer the case later in our time together, we both still preferred to address more important issues on paper.

In the beginning those issues centered on the friends she had left behind, the lost intimacies, the shortcomings of her new school. Melanie often read these entries aloud in class, a provocative announcement that she found Jones lacking on all counts and disdained what it offered. The net effect was to keep a lot of emotional doors shut tight to her as her classmates heeded the message of emotional distance.

From what I could observe, the main links Melanie was forging were with a group of boys who gathered at lunch to carry on an extended game of Dungeons and Dragons. They were an odd, misfit lot led by a charismatic, somewhat sinister young man aptly named Demon (DE-MONE). Melanie had a special affinity and understanding for people who were different, so these gatherings were an appropriate and convenient hedge against loneliness.

At the same time I felt myself being tested and measured against the supports that were available to her in the low moments at her previous school. With each written exchange, I could almost sense the invisible pass/fail grade being inscribed in the upper margin of my paper. In the best tradition of Holden Caulfield, students like Melanie have finely calibrated "shit detectors" whose alarm bells are easily activated by any hint of phoniness or insincerity. It is our loss that the sensitivity to genuineness, like our early acute sense of smell, atrophies with age in most of us.

Although I was never in school at the start of the day, the janitor always made sure to unlock my door first thing and make the room ready for my arrival. One day in that first fall I entered to find Melanie stretched out full length under the plant shelf by my window, the first of many times when she sought shelter in my room from the demons pursuing her, forcing her to flee her normal round of classes.

In a sense, this was my first hands-on test and here is my report card, delivered by Melanie the day after:

> Thank you for offering help and taking "no" as an answer. And though I'm fairly experienced in such manners thank you for not asking the two classic questions I hate! "Are you OK?" Nah—I lie sprawled on a cold floor, head buried in arms crying my body out as a way to show the world how happy and OK I am. "What's wrong?" Though more logical, less ignorant, and more helpful, still an awful

question. Too broad, too probing and never answered. One at that point is beyond simply telling right out what is wrong, only that something sure isn't right.

As the time approached for my first class to arrive, it became clear to me that it was not good either for them or for Melanie to find her in this dramatic pose. I kneeled beside her and suggested that I might find her another safety zone to which she could retreat.

> And thank you for a place where I could pull myself together and for writing a note. It was needed and apparently well-written, for the nurse was very kind and helpful after she read it. I didn't; my eyes were prisms. . . . The time was well used and much needed. I was able to answer my mother's question "How was school today?" with a calm, bored "Pretty good" with no problem and no question.

By avoiding a whole series of potential missteps I had passed a critical trust test with Melanie.

It is hard to explain how a student can be present and disappear at the same time, but this is exactly what Melanie did during the months after Christmas vacation. Long stretches passed during which I hardly noticed this otherwise vivid, flamboyant young woman. Earlier, the same person had taken over teaching my class and riveted everyone's attention in ways beyond my pedagogical reach through the use of candles, background music, and an innovative seating arrangement. Now even her handwriting was fading, moving from pen to pencil, ever more lightly applied, as if even violating the surface of the paper was an intrusion.

Busy teachers and harried parents often look back with shame at what they haven't been noticing—all the missed signals. Whatever the reason for my obtuseness, it took me weeks to realize that Melanie was sinking from sight. Her

academic work slowed to a trickle, and I suppose that's what
first caught my attention. It is also where the confusion of
roles between teacher and counselor came most sharply
into focus. As a teacher I must exact the penalties for non-
performance and then hurdle the desk to clasp the student's
hand and ask what the trouble is. That, in effect, is what
I did with Melanie in a note I left at her place in our odd
kidney-shaped arrangement of seminar tables.

Her reply came the next day, six pages of dim pencil, complete with time as well as date, as was often the case with her
letters. The hour was always shockingly late, a testimonial
to her troubled sleep.

1/16 ≈ 11:07 P.M.

Dr. Hoffman—
Yes, I've been rather to myself recently. A slipping back to
a time of great self-consciousness, of not wanting to give
anyone any weapon to my inner being. It took me a year at
PVA and a summer of freeness to get to a level area. Now I
feel myself slipping back, far back into a tunnel, the well of
total oblivion from the outside world. I've stopped writing,
stopped playing music, stopped caring about people or activities, or work of any sort. I do not want to be back where
I was. I'm trying to move forward, but it's only surfacely.
I'm forcing myself to get involved, to find something to
care about, some kind of motivation. I cannot lie to myself
nor can I force myself, bully myself into anything. I react
the same way a totally outside force would, I rebel, I become very stubborn and unmoving, I become sullen. I ache
very badly inside right now. The words blur as my eyes de-
bate whether to overflow or not. I am sad and feel terribly
defeated, the easiest of items are hard and impossible. I'm
sleeping poorly, but am always tired. When I do sleep, it is
haunted with demons of the night. I usually wake with a
wet pillow and an even heavier heart. I could barely get out
of bed this morning, finding it too much trouble, but mainly

not seeing any use in doing so. Had my mother been up, I would have stayed home. My father was, though, and I simply refused to talk to him unless directly spoken to. I spend as much time as possible alone, yet yearn for company. Everything is a task, the rewards are all gone. I cannot see the beauty in life anymore. I really do not want to do anything, simply want to hit a state of oblivion. I consider suicide, but cannot think straight enough of how to go about it. Earlier, I removed all sharp objects (I keep several bladed weapons) from my room and reach, just in case I hit a period of completely illogical thinking that I can remember nothing of later. Just a small item I remember from last year. I cannot speak to anyone, not that no one would listen or that no one would understand, for I know you will, as will a few others. Simply that my mind and mouth are really not on speaking terms, so to speak. I cannot express my mind through speech. I caught myself at a good time, the line from hand to mind is open, my thoughts are close to the word state.

Half the time I think nothing is wrong, I've just hit a rough bit. The other half, I feel 'tis deeper, that it may be getting serious, may be getting out of hand. Right now I feel the former. That's why I wrote my "symptoms" earlier. So you know the facts. I don't know how much more I can write. I do promise, however, to answer any response, in one form or another.

The letter is almost a textbook-perfect accounting of the symptoms of depression, and pre-suicidal thinking, though not one bit less poignant and wrenching for the pain it reflects. The remainder of the letter is a diatribe against her uncomprehending parents, who are, in turn, too oblivious, too self-absorbed, and too Pollyannaish to intuit her plight.

In the teacher-therapist role entanglement it is enormously difficult to sense when to step aside by letting students know that they need to seek help elsewhere. In spite of her trust in me and her willingness to be completely open, Melanie had an unerring sense of what was appropriate within overprescribed school roles. She wanted outside help as much as I insisted she needed it.

The problem was broaching that need to her parents. In spite of all the invective she heaped on them in her note, she was also inclined to protect them from knowledge of her trouble. Her mother's multiple sclerosis had been developing since Melanie was four, and she was now able to get to parent meetings and other school events only with the help of a little motorized cart. Her father's academic salary did not allow much margin for expensive professional help.

Nevertheless, I told her that if she didn't approach her parents with a request for help and an accompanying explanation of why she desperately needed it, then I would. Melanie made the move herself, partly out of desperation and partly from that inner core of strength and hunger to be whole that was sometimes masked by her depression.

Her mother called for suggestions of therapists, although her choices were limited by the constraints of her husband's health insurance. Her voice never lost its smiley, everything-is-moving-along-just-fine tone, although I had to wonder whether she didn't blame me for somehow forecasting these latest troubles.

After Melanie had broken the silence with her parents and set in motion the search for help, her depression bottomed out and she began showing signs of her old flamboyance and energy. The pencil gave way to a bold pen. Her movements were rapid and energetic. She was eating lunch with a new-found, older friend. Things definitely appeared to be on the upswing.

I was unprepared for the phone call from her mother informing me that Melanie was in the hospital. They had finally arranged an initial interview with a young psychiatrist who immediately recognized in her buoyancy a sign of new troubles, particularly when they were linked with the earlier suicidal reports. He recommended hospitalization and medication. All this the mother reported to me in the same relentlessly cheery tone in which she might recount a pleasant lunch with a friend. At least Melanie was being taken seriously. All along she had feared people would suspect her of exaggerating.

Melanie was gone for a month, the time fixed not so much by the pace of her recovery as by the terms of her insurance. We corresponded while she was in the hospital, but her definitive statement on the experience came later, when she could reflect back on it from a position of relative strength:

> In the hospital there was a unanimous feeling among us that if we could but be released, all would be well. That if we could pass the "test" here, we would be rewarded with ideal lives from there on out. It was especially strong among the weakest (of course). I felt then, as I still do now, looking back, that I was one of the strongest. I had the understanding of all the inner workings, and knew exactly how this all was set up. I knew what they wanted, what they were looking for. I knew what would get me out. I was far too intelligent for my own good. Also, however, since it was my idea to get help in the first place (more or less. Most of these ones were dragged in screaming and fighting by police or a carload of relatives.) I didn't want to have gone through all this for nothing. But the system, like most systems, worked considerably better in theory than in actuality. I found all the stress, depression, need for deception, and role of "I worry about others and ignore myself" greatly enhanced instead of decreased. If I am not mistaken, the main idea is to get the kids out of the environment that helped cause these problems in the first place into a sterile, well-controlled environment where they will feel safe and concentrate on their problems. It wasn't. I felt my physical safety threatened immensely and just about constantly. If you can't feel safe, you can't trust, you can't open, you can't work on anything but keeping your skin intact. I am not a group person. I am one that needs privacy, needs time to

myself, and enjoys one person's company at a time. Being in a group all my waking hours threatened to tear me apart on the very basic level of going insane from claustrophobia with the problems, emotions, lives of ten other people. It was a gang. Plain and simple. I was expected to fit into the group. O.K. I can do just about anything when I have to. I'd long ago achieved a state of "in but out," of being a part of the group while still being very separated. So I do. Except that I was not given the one item, the one basic right that I must have above anything. I do not expect to be liked, but I do expect, insist, to be accepted and respected as my own person. I have the right to believe what I wish, and to my own set of rules, morals, ideals, etc. I am not like anyone else and I refuse to act like everyone else. On this, I stood, stand, and will always stand firm. When someone is attacking my chosen way of life, saying that it is wrong, that it should be changed, I am the most stubborn thing. I am talking about the fellow inmates, and some of the staff nurses, not the doctors or therapists. It was this insistence, this refusal to give in to "the way of the gang" that utterly outcasted me, making me enemy. Anything that went wrong was blamed on me, from the inside. And they had their own ways to punish those enemies.

Despite this constant cat-and-mouse game (I played both, actually. Wasn't a purely defensive role that I played.), with my life and sanity for the prize, I did manage to do some work, some serious learning about myself. Which is why I am here writing this today, instead of decaying away in some plot of land. And I thought it was enough. I, too, had fallen into the trap of "everything is going to be just fine when I get out."

Of course everything was not just fine. Melanie had a shaky summer, including a long lonely stretch in Wisconsin, helping out during her grandmother's recuperation from a serious operation. Toward the end of the school year, Melanie had developed an intense relationship with another student whose emotional vulnerability and capacity for nurturance mirrored her own. The relationship sustained her through the difficult summer and a good part of the following fall.

Melanie managed to sculpt a schedule of electives for that second year that gave her at least one course with me each semester. Thus she was able to continue her beloved and constantly improving writing and to maintain an emotional anchor in her academic day that reinforced the support she was getting from her relationship with Danny. The hospitalization, for all that it lacked, had somehow convinced her that she really wanted to live, that she would not stand by passively while the undertow carried her away.

This new determination was underscored by a bizarre experience that became the subject of one of her best poetic efforts. One day she was walking along a bayou near her house when a gang of youths on the other bank fired a rifle at her without warning, without provocation. This completely arbitrary, absurd brush with death convinced her that she had no wish to die. That her life could end so abruptly for no reason filled her with outrage.

When I was first drawn to psychology, I was given to romantic visions of epiphanies, turnings in the lives of patients that were thoroughgoing and irreversible. Real life rarely yields up such gains. And that has been the case with Melanie. She still endures frightening lows, sudden crises. The relationship with Danny ended when he shifted his attachment to one of Melanie's best friends. As hurt and bereft as she was by this loss, Melanie managed to come through it with her friendship with Danny and his girlfriend intact, even strengthened.

Soon after breaking with Danny, Melanie began a new relationship with Paul, a recent transfer from a parochial high school. Paul was an attractive, intelligent, and sensitive young man. He and Melanie shared both an enthusiasm for writing and a history of emotional difficulties. Several months earlier he had been hospitalized after a suicide attempt that finally convinced his parents it was time to arrange his transfer from the rigidly restrictive parochial school. Melanie and Paul exchanged writings and intimacies in class and at lunch for some time, each serving the other during difficult transitions—she from Danny and he to his new school.

Then it was over and another difficult time began for Melanie. More than anything else she wanted out of her house. She couldn't abide the restrictions on her movements imposed by her parents. She hated the hollowness and hypocrisy of pretending to be a functioning and loving family when neither was the case. Her mother's physical condition was deteriorating and Melanie was carrying more of the household responsibilities. She took the longest possible route home from the school bus, delaying as long as possible her re-entry into that hated world. Sometimes she just curled up on a lawn on her way home and cried. Tears came often as she explored with me the dead-end prospects of finding a way out of her house now without having to wait almost a year and a half until college. The stopgap nights with friends and a spare bed in the University of Houston dormitory were not the answer.

But through all this, Melanie never crumbled, never talked about suicide. She could recognize this time that she needed professional help before things got any worse; she had to confront her parents with that need. She would have to face shattering her father's illusions that all her problems were behind her and her mother's anger and jealousy over drawing on the family's resources again to pay the fees, but she recognized that her very survival was at stake.

She never came to the same standstill in her work that had preceded the hospitalization. And she did not disappear. In fact, she was taking great pleasure in giving nourishment and support to others. In writing class she was discovering her gift for editing. In individual and small-group sessions others came to rely on her comments to guide them in revising their work. Her friend Julie was even needier than she during this period, and Melanie helped carry her through some frightening times, despite her own fragility.

Once again our work together seemed like a squatter's shanty, hammered together out of notes, letters, journals, poems, lunch hours, before-school meetings, dinners, car trips—not a conventional therapy hour among them. Melanie had been fortunate to have some of that kind of traditional help as well, but those therapists had been handicapped by their inability to see Melanie at her best, displaying her strengths as well as her pathology. And it is those strengths that kept her from sinking as low as she did the previous year.

I will let Melanie have the last word in this excerpt from an introduction to a poetry anthology she compiled on the subject of loss:

> Now, finally, I have learned how to keep my hands off the wound, to allow the time to heal, to let the healing do its job. To let the past be past and to accept the fact that I can do nothing for the past. I can only affect the here and now, the present. This is a tribute to what I am leaving behind.

CHAPTER 16

Julie:
I Ate the Source of My Inspiration

When Julie arrived for a lunchtime counseling session, she was not alone. She brought Melanie along for moral support. The pretext was that she wasn't sure what Melanie (who had brokered this meeting out of concern for Julie's suicidal thoughts) had already told me and didn't want to repeat herself. What the heck, I thought. It isn't what Freud prescribed, but if that's what it takes to get her through, so be it.

Very little in my professional training as a clinical psychologist prepared me for that lunch-hour encounter. Combat surgeons operate out of a field hospital after years of training in a pristine medical facility. Similarly, my mentors had never envisioned this brown-bagging violation of dearly cherished clinical principles. But this is the way it's been for years, since I assumed the hybrid role of classroom teacher and semiofficial school psychologist.

It was no accident that Julie had appeared in my room accompanied by Melanie. They were significant—and turbulent—forces in each other's lives, so Julie deserves her moment center stage. For me there are two Julies: the one she presented to me as her teacher; and the one she showed her "therapist." Even after years of training and experience I have to be reminded that the self others set out for public display is often no more substantial or sturdy than a two-dimensional Hollywood stage set.

In my first year at Jones I served as an adviser to the school literary magazine. Every Monday lunch hour I would sit with the prose editors to read and rate submissions for the once-a-year publication, which bestowed almost as much status on our literate population as participation in football does elsewhere. Julie's style in the editorial groups was tough and caustic. When she didn't like a submission, which was often, she slashed her way through the piece, pointing out weaknesses, deriding shallowness. This was done almost without drawing a breath, as if the lethal injection had to be administered with one steady thrust of the plunger.

Julie's appearance was as blunt and unadorned as her manners. Her uniform consisted of jeans, work shirt, and work shoes, a distinctly masculine statement on her broadly proportioned body. She wore no makeup, took no special care with her shoulder-length hair. This is who I am, her appearance said; if you don't like it, screw you.

In the fall of her senior year, Julie, a National Merit semifinalist, signed up for my creative writing class. Her primary goals were to finish a novel she had been working on for years, and to begin a fantasy work, based on an imaginary world she had created. Everything about the way she comported herself in class exuded an air of arrogance. She chose a table all to herself in our little circle and wrote through the whole period, ignoring presentations of work from her classmates, except for periodic slash and burn operations reminiscent of the literary magazine assaults. Julie never shared her writing with the class. She did show great hunks of it to me, but it was clear from her limited revisions that she was not overwhelmed by my suggestions. The novel's protagonist was a teenage boy severely brutalized and abused by his alcoholic father, who, unbeknownst to anyone except the boy, was also responsible for the death of the boy's mother. Structurally and linguistically it was the work of someone who had read widely, enough to have mastered an impressive range of vocabulary and literary devices.

I was surprised when Julie signed up for another of my electives the second semester. Her response to me seemed contemptuous, but I was not alone in that. Julie's tendency to refer to me and to her other teachers by no more than our last names ("Hoffman says . . .") without the softening introduction of a Mr. or Mrs. or Dr. carried a clear message about what she thought of us.

Julie appeared to be her usual prolific self—journals, poems, parts of stories—but I should have realized sooner that something was wrong. Nothing ever quite got finished. Plans laid out at the beginning of the week fizzled. She was becoming more elusive when I pressed her for work that I could comment on and help her revise. Her grades in other classes plummeted, forcing her to step down temporarily as literary magazine editor.

Which brings us to the unorthodox lunch-hour meeting with Melanie and Julie in my classroom. Melanie called me at home. She did this only when her personal situation was desperate, and even then only to make a date to see me in person at school. She disliked the phone as much as I did, and also maintained a keen sense of propriety about intruding on my personal life. This time the call was not for herself, but on Julie's behalf. She had spent the weekend at Julie's apartment, fearful about leaving her alone because there had been talk of suicide. The talk had reached that dangerous level of specificity where particular implements and methods are mentioned. Melanie was right to treat Julie's situation as serious.

This kind of hit-and-run counseling in combination with regular teaching responsibilities leaves little time for record keeping or note taking. As I recall, we discussed the suicide threats and the urgency of finding some professional help. I told her that I would be willing to see her for lunch-hour meetings in the meantime, but that this was only a stopgap. Her needs were too great and my relationship with her as teacher and extracurricular adviser were already too complicated to bear yet another layer.

Why did I agree to these meetings at all and why did I violate my own fundamental rule about contacting parents when there was even a hint of suicidal possibility? Julie was a wary and guarded person. She did not open herself to new relationships easily. Her attachment to Melanie was a real breakthrough and allowed an intimacy that existed nowhere else in Julie's life. On the several occasions during class when they asked permission to go off to a private place to talk, I granted that request. I risked being taken advantage of but was trusting Melanie not to betray my confidence.

Without Melanie's endorsement, Julie probably would have seen me as an untrustworthy adversary. That she would put herself in the hands of a complete stranger seemed highly unlikely to me, so in spite of my exhortations to seek *real* help elsewhere, I sensed that it was going to be me or nothing, at least during the three or four months that remained before graduation. So we conspired to share this convenient fiction that I was only holding the fort, knowing all the while that reinforcements were not on the way.

I don't know if Julie was actually already eighteen at this point, but it was clear to me that de facto she was no longer a dependent child. Julie's father had left so early that she did not remember him. From what I know of Julie's mother, she was the dependent partner in their relationship, and Julie worried about how her mother would fare when it was time for her daughter to go off to college. It was hard to see what benefit could come of bringing Julie's mother into the situation.

Something happened several weeks before our meetings began that, in retrospect, I can see broke an emotional log-jam and led up to the suicide threats and what followed. Julie's grandfather, a man with whom she had had little contact in recent years, died. Her reaction was out of proportion to the peripheral role this man had played in her life. He became the subject of a journal entry—the only one she volunteered to read aloud all year—a poem, and numerous references in classroom discussions. Somehow his death seemed to bring to the surface all that was missing, everything that had gone off course in her relationships. In our first session alone Julie spoke repeatedly of having decided around age thirteen that she was different, superior, and that she therefore needed to cut herself off from classmates, friends, family. She turned to writing, reading, listening to music. The novel she completed the previous semester probably had its start in that period.

Looking back, Julie realized that she had managed to paint herself into an emotional corner. She was lonely. She wanted love and friendships but the strategies she had developed for keeping people at bay were all too effective. No one wanted to venture too close to that fiery dragon's breath. Only one middle school teacher had managed to break through to win Julie's trust; beyond her lay an emotional wasteland.

In our second or third session together, Julie unloaded a bombshell that might have come as more of a surprise had I not already intuited it. From an early age, eight or nine, until her teen years, Julie's older brother had sexually abused her. They were alone in the house often, their mother off supporting them by working as a bookkeeper. For a long time,

Julie stopped trying to fight him off, realizing that the physical odds were against her. Resistance was possible only when she was older and stronger, enough of a physical match to make her threats to do him physical damage credible, and canny enough to use her verbal whip to disparage his sexual prowess.

It is a sign of our collective sickness that we can hear such stories and respond with a jaded ho-hum. Not another one. We should have known. My daughter once reacted to the all too familiar tale of a Holocaust survivor with a similar emotional yawn, and I could barely stop myself from leaping across the table to shake her.

The classroom was locked. In the halls the lunch crowd emitted an agitated animal sound. Soon the bell would ring and that beast would surge back into my classroom, leaving me and Julie no space for a transition from these dark revelations to the mundane world of grades and assignments. I admired Julie for the courage to entrust these secrets to me, particularly in such unpromising surroundings. She was matter-of-fact, unemotional in her telling, but the snarl was gone. Risking vulnerability had softened her, and although I was never fully comfortable with Julie, it was easier to see past the dragon who had first faced me across the table.

There was little anger directed at her brother for those years of brutalization. He lived in an apartment some miles away with a girlfriend, and Julie and her mother saw him often. One day before class Julie unpacked from her bag an Israeli army gas mask her brother had bought at an army surplus store. He was concerned that a part might be missing and Julie, aware of my knowledge of Hebrew, had offered to enlist my help in solving the mystery. Why had he bought such an object? How could Julie be helping this wretch who had stolen so much from her by brute force? Julie had learned to defend herself by compartmentalizing

her emotions, closing off the flooded compartments to keep
the whole ship from sinking. That was also how she was
able to avoid feeling any anger toward her mother, who had
failed in the ultimate parental responsibility of protecting
her child from harm.

There was plenty of anger all right—displaced, generalized.

Ode to a Bitch

I fell on my face
Helped on by your boot,
Burrowed down and wormed away.
It was the best thing I'd ever done;
The mud and animal shit
Were far kinder to my face (to me)
Than you ever were.

Another Fun Poem

By a maniac in a checkered blouse
With long hair and beaming green eyes
And no love of fallacy symbols.

Yes, it's another fun poem
that tickles your sides with razors
Rubbing your tummy with a wire brush
(Oh, how I'd love to walk on your back with *real*
Stiletto heels!)

Yep, another fun poem
for the sadists and masochists
who masturbate themselves and each other
with air-hammers.

Other poems were frontal attacks on male sexuality, not
unlike what she must have subjected her brother to, and
equally open paeans to the female sex organs and masturba-
tion. One set of these poems came with a note attached wondering whether the material bothered me. I wrote her back

that I was comfortable enough about my own masculinity to be able to look at the poems and judge them on their literary qualities, which were mixed. She also submitted some of these poems to the school literary magazine, where common sense and political exigencies made them unprintable, as Julie knew they would be.

Through these periods Melanie was deep into her relationship with Paul. Julie lost no opportunity in her writing to express her contempt for him. He was competition for Melanie's affections, and it was clear that Julie's attachment to Melanie went far beyond traditional friendship. Julie had no trouble acknowledging this. She considered herself bisexual, although it was never clear to me what experience, if any, she had had on either front. Altogether on her own during our sessions, Julie arrived at the insight that her attraction to women was linked to the abuse she had experienced at her brother's hands.

This epiphanic insight is the kind I spoke of earlier, the one I dreamed of as the culminating event that transforms the patient's life. Such is rarely the case. I suppose it was a step in getting control of an emotional life that had brought Julie to some disastrous impasses. But it could not negate the fact that riding close to the surface was a pervasive and corrosive sense of the meaninglessness of life that threatened to transform every event and every relationship into a hollow self-mockery. Looked at through one face of the prism, a situation might be fraught with significance; turn the prism one twist and it was all pointless.

Melanie was an important bridge to the outside world for Julie because she was on intimate terms with this existential vision. Although the intensity of the ties between them waxed and waned, they were able to hold on to each other without any complicated sexual ties, even after the end of Melanie's relationship with Paul. There was an asymmetry of need between the two; Melanie had emotional lifelines out in numerous directions, while Julie was investing everything in Melanie, but the imbalance was never exploited for cruel and hurtful purposes.

Being a National Merit semifinalist did not protect Julie against the senior-year panic over college admissions, which added yet another dimension to the year's turmoil. She had been somewhat cavalier about grades and applications. What if she had screwed up and would not be accepted anywhere? In her mind she carried the general outlines of a life plan— college, graduate school, and an academic career that would allow her the time and freedom to pursue her writing. If no one would have her now, not only would she be stuck at home, but her entire life plan would be derailed.

Acceptance notices from two respectable schools, one in a small academic community, one in a large, active city, eased the anxiety a bit. Now our discussions centered on the choices and the disagreement she and her mother were having over what might be best for Julie. Her mother demonstrated a great deal more worldliness and savvy than I had been led to expect by proposing that Julie secure places in both schools by mailing two deposits and then winning her over to the view that the larger, less isolated school suited Julie's needs better.

For all her intellectual sophistication and hard-bitten cynicism, Julie was an inexperienced and frightened little girl. She had been on her own very little and the prospect of college far from home—both choices were thousands of miles away—was daunting. It was in this direction that many of our final discussions turned. It was a *forward* turning, an anticipation of the future that stood in sharp contrast to the gloom of the early meetings where we seemed to be examining the question of whether there was to *be* a future. Julie was still in need of some kind of long-term help to explore the deeper wounds that were sure to open again under new stresses, but there was no denying that in our jerry-built relationship that was sometimes hard to recognize under the name therapy, we had moved to higher, safer ground.

From the time I first began teaching I introduced my students to a silly primitive ritual that took hold in such a powerful way that I have never abandoned it. It goes like this: On the first day of each month, on first seeing someone you must greet him or her by saying "Rabbit!" This ensures a month of good luck for both of you. In my classroom I solve the problem of having so many students to greet this way by writing "Rabbit!" on the board on that day.

On the first day of our last month together, I arrived in school to find that Julie had already come and gone off for some out-of-school appointment. When I pulled out my desk chair, I discovered that she had left a proxy—a little blue stuffed rabbit. No note. Just Julie's name. I don't think I've ever received a gift from a student in which the act of giving itself was so fraught with meaning. I have my doubts sometimes about the effectiveness of my work, but I think I earned this one.

In that last hectic week before graduation all semblance of a real schedule collapses for the seniors, so I never had another regular class with Julie. I barely saw her long enough to thank her for the rabbit and promise that I would display it at the first of every month from here on in. She responded with a smile I had never seen before, a sunny, uncomplicated little girl's glow of pure satisfaction.

I saw her once more, at graduation, on the steamy steps of a university auditorium, a scorching summer afternoon reserved only for hell and Houston. Julie wore her yellow robe over some disreputable outfit—it must have been shorts and a T-shirt—a final opportunity to thumb her nose at the establishment. We gave each other a big hug. I don't think it was lost on either of us that in our decorous professional dealings there had never been the slightest physical contact between us. Like the rabbit, this too signaled how far we had come.

One more thing. I was, after all, still Julie's teacher. In that capacity I need to report that in the end, she was able to pull together a most interesting and unusual anthology of poetry interspersed with a running commentary addressed to me. The poems had been worked over, revised, taken seriously. There were the harsh, venomous pieces I included here, but there was more. Here is a final poem, unburdened of the negative weight of the earlier poems, yet perhaps concealing an emotional significance deeper than its flashier counterparts.

Here's one I don't know if I showed you or not. It was inspired by a Cheese Puff that looked like a beckoning finger.

I Ate the Source of My Inspiration

I looked at it
Pondering
For a moment
Questioning its appearance
Its implications
Symbols
Felt my mind grasp
At an inspiration
The first words
of an idea.
I considered
Toying with a twinkle
Chasing the idea
Onto my paper
Planting it on the first line
And seeing what grew

Across the page—
Then I ate it.
Its image inspired my mind
More than its taste
inspired my tongue.
Then I wrote a poem about it.

For me, that's the last word on therapy and teaching.

CHAPTER 17

Arthur:
The Pearl in the Oyster

I lost Arthur somewhere along the way this year. No teacher with messianic pretenses likes to own up to such a loss, and it wouldn't be nearly as painful if I hadn't convinced myself that I had "found" him earlier. There are kids you never get to. You go through the motions with them, yet in spite of your best efforts and most practiced ploys, they never let you in. When you see them in the hall the next semester it's hard to call up their names on your mental computer screen. But with Arthur I felt like I had dug down to life-giving water, only to watch the source dry up so decisively that even traces of the well were gone.

When I scan the room on the first day of school, I play a little game with myself: which of my first impressions are going to be upended this year? Arthur, for one, exuded a steely ferocity that looked unapproachable. He was five feet eleven inches tall, very solidly built, hair cropped close to expose the contours of his skull like a survey map. He dressed in fashionable European-style shirt and pants that billowed at the upper arms and hips and narrowed at the wrists and ankles. Arthur's skin was coal black, so black he almost glistened. When he smiled, exposing his perfect teeth, the contrast of enamel against skin was stunning. But there weren't many smiles early on—just a wary opacity. The first impression was not promising.

Among the half-formed boys in this sophomore class, Arthur stood out—an adult in a world of children. I didn't know that first day that he was almost twenty, and even when things opened up a bit between us I never learned precisely where all those lost years had gone. I knew there was a semester lost to jail, time served in the juvenile detention center following a stabbing: "I wasn't always as big as I am now, and I had to carry a knife to defend myself," Arthur explained. Add to that lost time for truancy and for assorted course failures and the sum is the discouraging prospect of graduation from high school at an age when your suburban-reared counterparts are contemplating medical school.

The early Arthur seemed an unapproachable block of obsidian. I believe that a good teacher, endowed with the proper degree of enthusiasm, wisdom, decency, openness, and love can go a long way toward overcoming differences between himself and his students, but sometimes I wish it was easier. If only the kids slouched in their chairs before me had all grown up on my old block and hung out in front of my own corner candy store, then the cultural code of their lives in all its nuances would come clear. There was no way this goody-goody Ph.D. teacher who carried a knife of the Swiss army variety—only to cut package strings and open beer bottles— was going to penetrate fully the world in which knives were for self-defense.

The first hint that obsidian too has many facets came when we began writing journal entries several days a week. The writing time was usually not more than ten minutes, after which I invited volunteers to read their entries to the class. In most classes the invitation to read is accepted by a few habitual exhibitionists and a rolling sample of others who are in crisis or who have perpetrated something extremely rich and funny that cries out for an audience.

From the beginning the response was different in Arthur's class. When I announced the end of the ten-minute writing time it was like popping the cork on a champagne bottle. Hands went up everywhere begging to read. There were many days when I never got to the lesson plan I had crafted for the day. I felt guilty and uncomfortable about not moving ahead with the plans until I realized that the curriculum was right there in front of me. The students were writing, talking, responding to one another, building a community, and they were inviting me to come along. I just had to relax and let it happen.

Arthur was always one of the first to volunteer. When he read, he commanded attention. His voice was a rich baritone and his language flowed with the cadences of good music. He didn't write intimate self-revelatory entries. They were more like personal position papers, sermonettes on the relationship between men and women; the pride of the black man; the nature of friendship. His closest encounter with personal revelation was a report of listening to a recording of a popular gospel group that had inspired him to move closer to God. I could hear snickers of disbelief from his classmates. Somehow godliness was not one's first association with Arthur. The writing was flawless technically, smooth and clear in style. From where I sat on my padded stool I could look over at Arthur's paper and appreciate even further his quest for style, for the grand gesture. The page was its own work of art— covered with a backslanted script punctuated by symmetrical curlicues, upturned embellishments at the end of each word. What Arthur produced, in both its written and its oral presentation, was pure strutting performance, intended to be admired. Performance was the leitmotiv of Arthur's life.

I was praising Arthur's productions, hoping that my reinforcement would maintain the flow, but there still wasn't much connection between us. His audience was his classmates. It was from them that he sought favor and attention.

I was out of class one day in late October, and when I got back I found a note in my box. Arthur had withdrawn from school and in my absence somebody had signed him out of my class, a bureaucratic formality involving textbook return and initialing of various withdrawal documents. I was shocked. Here was a guy who needed to graduate and go to college; he had all the verbal tools to succeed there. I dug out his registration card and copied his grandmother's phone number. I knew his parents were out of the picture. In an early letter of introduction, Arthur had provided me with a complete family history. "My father is no good and my mother is strung out." Period.

His grandmother was as astonished as I was by the news of his withdrawal. As far as she knew, Arthur had left for school yesterday and today, catching a ride as he always did with his homeboy Praygene, who lived upstairs. He never said a word about quitting, dropping out. She admitted that it wasn't easy for her to keep up with Arthur, particularly since she was disabled and didn't get out of the house much. She would check upstairs with Praygene's mother and call back later if she learned anything further.

Arthur was in my classroom waiting when I returned from the phone call. I guess he had come to say good-bye, a rare gesture from any of my dropouts, who tend to just evaporate, like smoke. But before he had a chance to explain himself, I unloaded on him the story of the note, my concern, my call to his grandmother. "You called my grandmother. Oh, man, I can't believe you called my grandmother." He played that line back as he ran his hand across his close-cropped scalp, as if to clear his head. I had obviously complicated his plans by blowing his cover. He hadn't quite figured out how to ease his grandmother into the news that he was intending to quit, to move on, to get a job that would support him better than his part-time hours at Eckerd Drugs. What about school, I asked? Arthur said he was going to try to take the GED, so he could get his diploma and go to college. He was getting too old for this high school business. Kevin, another bright student who outgrew high school, checked out last year with the intention of getting a GED. It was like the after-life; no one ever returned to tell the tale. I had my doubts.

Arthur seemed mad at me for intruding on his life, and I had to intrude even further by reporting the latest chapter to his grandmother when she called back later. The next day Arthur was back in his regular seat, without any explanation of the sudden return to the status quo beyond the fact that he had changed his mind. During a year of journal writing and truncated conversations, the story of Arthur's amazement that I had cared enough to call home, that I was upset by his departure, emerged. This simple gesture was enough to draw him back to school. It made me feel ashamed for all the calls I hadn't made, all the kids who had slipped through the very rough mesh without a murmur of protest or concern from me. Most of them hadn't shown me enough to make me care. I hate the telephone, do everything I can to avoid calls home in any case, but how many kids might have been turned around by a call from me and from all those teachers who preceded me in their lives? There are families and kids out there who would have been moved to know that they were not invisible, that they were counted an asset in someone's ledger.

Arthur repaid me in his own currency, by letting me into a small corner of his out-of-school life. He told me to tune in to one of the local black radio stations at seven-thirty that Friday night. There would be a surprise. I followed his instructions and there he was, his unmistakable voice emceeing the show together with a group of his homeboys who took turns breaking out into raps of their own creation. It sounded fairly polished although I had my usual decoding problems.

On Monday morning he gave me a pop quiz to see whether I had done my homework. He was pleased to learn that I had heard the show and approved of his performance. He was signaling that it did matter to him what I thought. I was now a recognized and legitimate part of his audience.

Showing care and concern is, as the logicians say, a necessary but not sufficient condition for learning. Arthur and his classmates still needed to be introduced to books and ideas that would excite and engage them and that appeared to be connected with what they saw of life. With Arthur's class I had decided from the beginning to wander even further from the textbook and the standard curriculum than I normally do. I am not a textbook teacher by inclination in any case, but in the first years of working with my "regular" high school classes, I succumbed to timidity and clung to the textbook for at least half the year. As textbooks go, ours is not a bad one. It is sprinkled with the obligatory number of minority writers and the balance between contemporary and earlier works certainly beats the classical and nineteenth-century-laden works of my school years. Still, we are confronted with the formidable task of making Stephen Crane and *Medea* and *Our Town* play in the South Park ghetto of Houston.

In fact I have been able to breathe life into these works for my black students, but the effort strains my ingenuity to the breaking point. Each of these works has a universality that justifies its place among the classics. In *Medea* jealousy and revenge unfold against the backdrop of a mother's love for the children she cruelly sacrifices. There are mothers in my classroom who can connect with Medea's anguish. And there are kids who can see in *Our Town*'s portrait of life and death in a small town some link with the rural hamlets where they have drifted through sleepy summers with their grandparents.

There are compelling arguments to be made for reaching for this universality and deductively tying it to the black world of my students. This year I wanted to reverse the flow, to move inductively from literature rooted in the black world to the larger issues that affect and afflict all of humanity. All great literature is rooted in the specific—in Yoknapatawpha County or Macondo or St. Petersburg.

So we began in the housing projects of Brewster Place and lived with, read about, and discussed Gloria Naylor's cast of single mothers, black activists, rural transplants, and gay black women. Alongside our reading students wrote about their own neighborhoods and some of the interesting and unusual characters who inhabit them.

> In my neighborhood, there is no peace and quiet. When I get up in the morning I see kids selling dope and drugs, which is not nice at all. . . . My neighborhood is okay. It's just that when you need some peace, you can't get it. You just have to go right along with the game.

> And on the right side of my street from my house, a man lives in a red and yellow house. He has three big brown dogs. Every time someone walks by his house they bark very loudly. Sometimes I walk across the street just to make them bark.

Many of the kids had seen *The Women of Brewster Place* on television, which anointed the material with legitimacy that does not reside in mere books. This was the stuff of their lives and the lives of people they knew.

From here we moved on to drama. I took my cue from the

students' obvious pleasure in reading out loud the work we were studying. I had already noted Arthur's dramatic flair during journal time and was determined to find a way for him and several of his histrionic classmates to spread their wings. We began with the traditional favorite, *A Raisin in the Sun*, and followed the dramas of Mama and Walter, Ruth and Beneatha through their troughs and peaks. We watched Sidney Poitier fall and rise again in the film version, then parceled out the roles and worked through some of the critical scenes ourselves. Although there is still a lot for students to connect with in Hansberry's work, it has begun to fray for me. It feels dated and moralistic, a bit too pat in its perceptions of race and family. The memory of George Wolfe's wicked parody of *Raisin* and similar works of the 1960s and 1970s that he labels "Mama on the Couch" plays in his revue *The Colored Museum* makes it difficult to read Mama or Walter's monologues as Hansberry intended.

We hit our stride with *Fences* by August Wilson. In this gritty portrait of Troy Maxson, an angry, frustrated ex-baseball player turned garbage man, we heard language so real and familiar to the students that they could not read a page without chuckles of amused familiarity: Troy and Bono exchanging raunchy comments on the ripeness of Florida women, or Troy being hustled by his ne'er-do-well son Lyons for a loan. They were so surprised to hear their own voices and rhythms represented on the page that they often attempted to "correct" the language by translating it back into standard English during our readings, as if there were something improper about their dialect being honored in serious literature.

Arthur's readings of Troy were so popular that my democratic attempts to rotate the parts through the class met with resistance. People wanted Arthur to *be* Troy. He captured the seething, frustrated anger of the man thwarted in his own ambitions, determined not to see his son hurt the same way, and selfishly seeking comfort in another woman at the expense of his loyal wife.

During the weeks we devoted to *Fences*, Arthur rarely missed a day. His engagement spilled over into his writing, which had never been more intense and articulate. The students were preparing for a statewide writing proficiency exam that called for a well-organized persuasive essay. The guidebook for teachers prepared by a panicky school district staff, fearful of drowning under an avalanche of failing scores, offered well-meaning suggestions for exercises, such as "write a letter to your principal arguing for a change that would improve your school." In the course of searching for meatier fare, I showed the class a television interview with August Wilson, the author of *Fences*, in which he attacks *The Cosby Show* as a damaging distortion of black life in America. I taped some *Cosby* episodes and we viewed them together in class. Then we wrote. First, I asked them to imagine that they were visitors from another world who knew nothing of black people other than what they had seen on *The Cosby Show*. What could they say about family life? Relations between the sexes? Relations across the generations? Then I asked them to takes sides on whether the *Cosby* version of black life was constructive or damaging for black people. Arthur dissected Cosby's black world with an anthropologist's canniness. He advocated passionately the need for positive models for black people to emulate and aspire to, even if they did not represent the current reality of most members of the community.

> *The Cosby Show* in my opinion is not unrealistic. To label this show as being unrealistic means it's "impossible to achieve." Stereotyping has been a big part of the black race. What people want to see is the black man committing adultery, the black woman on welfare, the black children

selling drugs or pregnant. *The Cosby Show* has views that I
think young children or even adults should want to follow
and bring forth as being realistic.
The show is heart warming.
Is that unrealistic?
It's loving.
Is that unrealistic?
It's showing values.
Is that unrealistic?
It's showing you how to strive and fight for what you want.
Is that unrealistic?
It's showing you how to keep an open mind.
Is that unrealistic?
It's showing you how to be aware.
Is that unrealistic?
It's showing you that there are other things out there besides
drugs, sex, and violence that are going to challenge till
death.
Is that unrealistic?
If you think that parents who love their children and sacri-
fice, who love each other enough not to argue and fight
is not real, then what kind of parent or spouse will
you be?
The future is where we have to live and raise our children.
Why not make this real? Why not make this our life?

Then I lost courage. Through the long, exciting months of
Brewster Place, *Raisin*, and *Fences*, my students continued
lugging their oversized purple textbooks to class, though we
never used them. They clung to the books for security, talis-
mans that assured them this really was an English class although none of the proceedings seemed familiar from past
experience. Okay, I said, maybe it's time for something more
"universal" from the textbook, but at least it's got to be
whole. Nothing excerpted, nothing fragmentary.

Textbook publishers are herd animals, following slavishly
one behind the other. All have adopted the practice of

including one full-length novel in their anthology. For our book the choice was Steinbeck's *The Pearl*, the work of a serious, respected author, but not great literature.

The class included repeaters and students who had transferred from other teachers midyear. Demetria and a few others had read *The Pearl* in other classes, and she trumpeted the news that she had found it boring while I engaged in teacherly damage control. Since I had cultivated openness and honesty, I could hardly chide Demetria for speaking her mind, but I did suggest that it was "different strokes for different folks," that not everybody would love every book on the reading list. We barely survived *The Pearl* on the credit that I had banked with the class over the year.

I had reached the inevitable flat spot in the year when energy flags and teaching goes on automatic pilot for a time, even in the best of classes. We still had our raucous journal days, and even our encounter with *The Pearl* had its moments. One day I set up a role-playing situation, specifically aimed at drawing Arthur back into some engagement. He had entered into a decline that had me puzzled. Now Arthur was the callous town doctor who first refuses to treat the scorpion-bitten child of a peasant couple, then changes his tune when the circumstances change through the discovery of the pearl. He was by turns arrogant, unctuous, underhanded, and stony, much to the delight of his classmates.

During our work on *Fences*, I had suggested to Arthur that he find some place to develop his acting talent. He had done some stage work at another high school before transferring here, but our school had no active drama program. There are three areas in high school that have visible products whose quality can and will be judged by the outside world—drama and performance, publications (yearbook, newspaper, literary magazine), and sports. Only sports and a literary magazine exist in our school. The absence of the other activities is a drag on school morale, and we are caught in a vicious cycle of disengagement.

Arthur posed the obvious question to me: where, then, could he turn to pursue his acting? He had never been to a play, had no knowledge of the existence of amateur and professional groups in the city. He needed the kind of leg up that middle-class parents provide in their constant quest for options and opportunities for their children. Here was my opportunity for Messianic Intervention: if I opened the right door for Arthur he could be saved.

I called a friend, Thomas Meloncon, a highly reputed black playwright whose children attend our school, and told him about Arthur. Thomas had come up the hard way himself and had gotten a few breaks. He understood the messianic impulse and volunteered to come in to talk with Arthur himself.

I don't know what Arthur expected from the encounter, but he was excited when I told him what I had arranged. I've discovered in the past that often my students don't understand how many steps lie between them and their dreams—steps involving drudgery and hard work. Perhaps he expected a lead role in a local production. Instead what happened was that Meloncon made a pre-arranged appearance at my classroom door and I dispatched Arthur to the hall to meet with him.

Meloncon exhorted Arthur to stay in school if he was serious about acting and suggested he work up some tryout monologues so he would be prepared to respond to casting calls as companies around the city announced them. Arthur seemed high after the talk and borrowed several books of monologues I had gathered in the class library.

Psychologists are masters at imagining spurious connections among probably unrelated events. Arthur's decline began a week or two after his meeting with Meloncon. Was it somehow related to a fear that after all of the posturing about being famous one day, he wasn't really up to the challenge of acting? Or perhaps the long string of absences that unwound opposite Arthur's name in my roll book were linked to the doldrums into which our classroom had fallen. In fact the source of what was driving him down must have been elsewhere—far beyond the limited line of vision I had on Arthur's life.

Whatever the cause, watching the proud Arthur's decline during those last months of the school year was painful. His dignity was drifting further and further from shore as I stood on the beach, my calls to return ever more inaudible. He was cutting my class. His classmates reported sightings of him during the day, but come fourth period Arthur's chair was empty. On a rare day when he did appear, he got into an ugly round of ranking with Moretta, who was in no mood to be messed with herself. She was preoccupied with an impending trial on a robbery charge. Arthur was downright belligerent and the two fell just short of duking it out right there in class. I missed all the cues that the students recognized immediately. Arthur was drunk. I had seen friends grow surly and combative when they were drinking, but even the most savvy teacher can overlook the symptoms of schooltime drinking.

On another day, Arthur put his head down on the table during journal writing and did not commit a single word to paper. Perhaps he was drunk again—or stoned—but it felt more as if he was sinking under a weight of meaninglessness. The fall's reprieve from dropping out had expired and Arthur was once again overcome with the hopelessness of his academic situation. It was an endless cross-country drive that would never bring him to the coast.

The gaps in Arthur's attendance meant that even when he came and managed to stay awake, he was out of the flow.

I seldom heard his rich baritone voice because without read-ing or participating in the preliminaries he had nothing to contribute. He just looked on bemusedly, like a child who has detached himself from his surroundings to cushion the blow of an impending move.

It was too painful to think about ending the year with Arthur in silence. I stopped him after class one day during the last week to tell him how sad and disappointed I was that things hadn't turned out better and that I was bewildered about what had gone wrong. It was then he confessed to his involvement with the "wrong crowd." Was it a sop to him-self or to me that he told me he planned to reinstate his dor-mant GED plans along with his intention to head for the campus of the local black college?

Someone who had come up out of Arthur's world might have read the cues more quickly and accurately. They might have pulled him through. But there are not enough ex-Arthurs teaching in our schools. Enlisting the powerful spir-its of Troy Maxson, Walter Younger, and the women of Brewster Place was the right idea, but in the end they are ghosts, of limited help in bailing water from the sinking dinghy that is Arthur's life. Those of us who temporarily share that boat must row and bail furiously, hoping against hope that it will stay afloat long enough to come to rest on some life-saving reef.

CHAPTER 18

Monica:
Can We Be Friends?

When the lunch bell rings, the kids deploy to their battle stations. Most of the "regular" kids head for the cafeteria, where only the hearty thrive amidst the noise, the jostling, the mating dances. The newly installed Pizza Hut snack wagon draws the largest crowd of foragers. Some of the Vanguard kids flock to the inner courtyard with whatever remains of their snack lunches, most of which have by now been surreptitiously consumed in class. It's a long way between the breakfastless bus boarding at six in the morning and the noon lunch hour. The rest fan out to various classrooms where accommodating teachers offer asylum to crowd-shy students and those with last-minute homework assignments to subdue. These rooms are also safe havens for students with special interests they can't pursue after school because of the long cross-city bus rides awaiting those too poor or too young to have their own wheels.

The chessboards are operational in Mr. B's room; in Madame's class, kids are preparing for the statewide French competition; in Ms. J's class, the literary magazine editors are meeting to compile the final selections for this year's issue.

My room draws the odd lots—the last-minute-homework contingent, the fantasy-game players still in search of a permanent home and mentor, and the loners who have no steady peers with whom to break candy bars.

Monica is a fixed star in my lunchtime firmament. She parks her ample frame at one of my tables almost every day, a tradition extending back more than two years now. There is nothing forlorn or pathetic about her aloneness. She has friends. From time to time she banters with classmates in the various groups scattered around the other tables. But on most days she prefers to read or to talk with me. On any given day her reading might consist of John Grisham or Tim O'Brien.

"I just love Grisham. His stories are so great. I can't put them down."

"It's fine for you to read those books, Monica. I'd probably read more of them if I were a faster reader, but I have to reserve my reading time for real literature," I respond.

"You're really a snob about writers like Grisham, but I know what you mean. I like those books in a different way. Writers like Tim O'Brien are trying to do something with language. Still . . ."

It's taken some effort on both our parts for Monica to arrive at this formulation of the difference between escape reading and literature. Try hawking this distinction to someone who doesn't already share your predilections and you'll see how hard it is to communicate what sets enduring art apart from airport books.

When Monica asks for book recommendations, she declares that she's willing to read anything I suggest so long as it's written in what she refers to as "regular English"—a category that excludes the likes of Shakespeare, Dickens, and Twain.

But mostly we don't talk books. I sip my daily dose of Slim-Fast from the Mason jar in which I have mixed it the night before and eat my prescribed green apple, core and all—to Monica's disgust. When she ran out of patience with my cumbersome jar, she presented me with a plastic bottle with built-in sipping straw; if it didn't make its daily appearance, she would be hurt. She picks through a bag of M&M's, avoiding all the greens, or eats a red apple, if it hasn't turned too soft for her taste. Monica's lunches may not be balanced, but they're also not gargantuan, certainly not enough to explain how overweight she is. She has a pretty face with a cupid bow mouth and is one of those fortunate heavy people who are able to carry their weight gracefully, even in shorts, so that no one would ever dream of feeling sorry for her or treating her with derision.

In one of our earliest conversations between sips and munches during her junior year, she commented on the posters and books I had laid out for the Holocaust project then in process in my senior English class.

"I can't understand how anybody could do what the Nazis did to the Jews. I've read a lot of books about it, but it really doesn't make any sense."

Since Monica had borrowed from me a photographic essay about German settlers in nineteenth-century Texas, I knew that there was a strong Germanic ingredient in her own family mix. What drew her so inexorably to the Holocaust was the discovery of Nazi skeletons in her closet.

"There were actually some real Nazis in my family in Germany, and it's like, I'm responsible in some ways for what they did."

For me, the defining moment in our Holocaust study, the experience that lifts it from the page and the celluloid and demands that we confront the horror directly, revolves around the visit of a survivor. Every year I invite one of the several hundred survivors living in Houston to my classroom to bear witness.

I knew how much it would mean to Monica to hear this year's visitor, a personal friend, born in Holland. Chaja was taken by the Nazis at age three from the hiding place arranged by her parents and was liberated two years later, one of the rare child survivors of the concentration camps. I armed Monica with a note for the fifth-period teacher requesting that she be allowed to join us on the day of Chaja's visit. And there she was, in her same lunch-hour seat, but this time surrounded by seniors who had been living with the Holocaust for the past month.

Monica sat impassively through Chaja's talk and the questions that followed. It may have been my imagination, but her eyes seemed moist. At the end, Monica volunteered to escort Chaja through the confusing maze of hallways to the parking lot. I never asked her what passed between them on that walk, but I sensed from her bearing that somehow she had begun the process of expiating the sins of her family, committed by people she never knew.

My own Jewishness is part of what draws Monica to me, not just because of the Holocaust, but because she herself is a devout Christian. Our differences intrigue her, something more complicated than *opposites attract*. Instead, it's fueled by a fascination with how the other half thinks.

She is far more sophisticated than the students who are aghast at the idea that I, along with the majority of people on the face of the planet, do not accept Christ as our savior. Although this belief is central to her very being, Monica does not declare me doomed to hell. She just keeps probing, questioning.

"Just what do you believe that's different from us? Do you accept that Jesus was real? Do you believe in heaven?" Deceptively simple questions requiring extraordinarily complex answers. I'm not sure whether my answers offend or intrigue her, but they never close down our dialogue.

Our religious differences pale next to our political disputes. Monica's favorite lunch-hour pastime is disseminating the latest Bill Clinton jokes she has collected from wherever such gems emanate. By her standards I am a liberal, and that is far more heinous than being Jewish because the latter is, after all, imposed by birth.

"Can you believe that idiot Clinton blaming the Oklahoma bombing on talk show hosts? Give me a break!"

"Come on, Monica, you don't think that Liddy giving instructions on how to shoot federal agents is an incitement to violence?"

Monica may not be a flat-out Limbaughite, but she shares many of his hard-line views on big government and its encroachments on individual rights. A typical lunch-hour joust opens with "Can you believe . . . ?" followed by the latest bit of governmental absurdity, ineptness, or heavy-handedness gleaned from the television news—an unnecessary foreign aid grant, an intrusive environmental regulation, all grist for her ideological mill.

Although "bleeding heart" would be a pejorative term among many of her political allies, Monica's heart bleeds in certain predictable areas. She loves small children. Their innocence, helplessness, and vulnerability touch her deeply. In her senior year she has settled on attending a small church-affiliated college in Arkansas where she intends to prepare herself to teach young children. I have never seen her happier than the day she brought to school the news that she had been hired to work as a counselor in a summer children's program. Apart from the usual round of baby-sitting, this will be her first formal opportunity to pursue what she considers her calling. Newt Gingrich's proposed cuts in education and other children's programs do not sit well with

Monica, whose own brand of conservatism does not include punishing or ignoring society's underdogs.

Monica's own pedigree does not place her among the elite. It never was clear to me how her father earned a living, but it wasn't much of one in any case. The family's financial straits drove Monica and her mother at one point to take on a late-night janitorial job in a Houston office building. Some time around ten o'clock each night they would begin their round of basket emptying, toilet swabbing, vacuuming, and sweeping. This nocturnal ritual netted them about fifteen dollars, hardly enough to salve the wounds to their egos.

Their house seemed to be falling apart around them. For a long time Monica complained about the fact that she hadn't had a good warm shower in weeks. The pipes were broken and her father was either too lazy or too broke to fix them. After a particularly intense rainstorm that flooded many Houston streets and turned cars into floating river barges, the roof on parts of Monica's house collapsed and water ruined many of the family possessions.

She is, by turns, angry, pissed off, resigned. She wonders whether she can hold out long enough to make her escape to college, out from under a father so inept and so unreasonable that his refusal to file income tax returns jeopardized the submission of financial aid forms that were her ticket to the loans and grants she so desperately needed.

There are hints of darker secrets involving her father, but Monica has admitted in our lunch-hour chats that until she felt more steady, it was better to defer creating new waves. Monica is no innocent. Her conversation is filled with references to friends who have succumbed to drugs, drinking, and early promiscuity. I have the impression that her attraction to religion is woven from a combination of those dark familial secrets and her observations of the ravaged lives of her peers.

In an essay she wrote in my English class about the teachers at Jones who had left their mark on her, she included a section on me, in which she said that what she valued in our relationship had all the qualities of a good friendship. That's not to say that I was trading intimacies with her tit for tat, but it did mean that she could disagree, argue, fulminate without fear that I would pull rank on her. In the midst of one of our political and religious exchanges I was not likely to say, "Now, young lady, this has gone far enough. You need to remember where you are and whom you're addressing." Such sail trimming was never really necessary because Monica never crossed any invisible boundary of impropriety with me.

Those boundary lines are drawn differently by different adults, and the teachers and administrators who were put off by her accused her of everything from hysteria to witchcraft.

When we speak of diversity, we are usually referring to the student population in a school and the virtues of students engaging with peers of different backgrounds. No one could have been more different than Monica and I were on every imaginable scale. Yet we were enriched by those teacher-student friendships across political, religious, and social class lines. The virtues of diversity transcend generational boundaries, as do the possibilities of friendship. It's no accident that I count at least a dozen former students among my friends today. Age differences tend to implode when they are stripped of the trappings of institutional roles. All the more so when those seeds were encouraged to sprout from the outset.

CHAPTER 19

Kathy:
Reaching for the Light

Doug is one of the regulars on the Jones High School maintenance crew. I meet up with him almost every morning when I make my late appearance in the building in the middle of third period. The halls are empty, allowing Doug an unobstructed path to slide his oversize dust mop down the locker-lined hallway, capturing paper scraps and lunch box droppings like a foraging animal.

When he finishes his rounds he stops by my room to visit with the plants I've crowded onto the window ledges to mask the cinder block coldness of my spartan classroom. Sometimes Doug brings me a cutting from a plant he has recently pruned at home, like the pencil cactus that rests on its own stool by the window, its place of honor ensured. Together we chart its progress, speculating about how high up the wall it will reach by spring. Every growing thing that Doug passes his hand over thrives in spite of the long school vacations, droughts, breakdowns of heating and cooling systems, and mischievous student assaults; when summer vacation begins I won't hesitate to leave all my plants in his care.

That charmless building is not promising soil for either

plant or child, and I wish that my rate of success with students was as good as Doug's with plants. Yet even in the rocky garden that I tend there are amazing, almost unaccountable examples of growth and resilience. In many ways they make a more interesting, less told tale than the battle stories about our schools that circulate regularly.

Kathy's life story is a prescription for disaster. If she succumbed we would nod our heads knowingly, recognizing the tragic inevitability of failure. Here is her own account, extracted from the essay that accompanied her college applications.

Remembering . . .

It's just like the old saying that you can't understand how someone feels until you've been in his shoes. Now at the age of eighteen as I walk the streets of downtown Houston, I understand the feelings of the men and women who are slumped against buildings to hide from the cold. I feel that unlike the majority of the people hurrying into big office buildings or hopping into cars, I am able to relate to these homeless people.

Today I am a senior in an accelerated high school program for gifted and talented students and will graduate near the top of my class. I am involved in several activities in school, including a statewide French competition in which I placed first in poetry and prose and second in prepared speech two years ago. But my life was not always so promising.

I can remember when my mother had a job and every other week when she received her paycheck, we would walk to the supermarket and come home with five or six bags of groceries. We had a small, decent apartment which was just the right size for me, my little sister, and my mother. Rough times did occasionally fall upon us, especially after my mother was fired from her job. I still remember the time we had to go without electricity for ten months. At night my mother would plug an extension cord into an outlet in the hallway and run it into our living room. Eventually the landlord caught on and had a big falling out with my mother. Then one night, totally unexpected, two men from a Catholic church walked up to our door and handed my mother a two hundred dollar check, with which she paid the electric bill. Not too long after this our rental manager threatened to evict us because we were having trouble paying the rent. My grandmother sent him four hundred dollars to catch up on the back rent that we owed, but it wasn't enough because less than a week later the Harris County Sheriff's Department was banging on our door at seven o'clock one Saturday morning, demanding that we be off the premises by twelve P.M.

We spent three months in Maryland with my grandmother while my mother unsuccessfully looked for a job, but then my grandmother sent us back to Houston. We arrived at ten o'clock one night with exactly one penny to our name. I was only ten years old at the time and my sister was only three, and all either one of us understood was that we didn't have any money.

Thanks to a man working in the train station we found out that the Greyhound Bus Station stayed open all night. We were there for a week until the police came and told us to leave or be thrown in jail. With shopping bags full of our few remaining belongings, we camped out on benches in shopping centers, and stayed with strangers who would take us in for a night. Someone finally told us that Harris County Welfare would find us a place to stay. This started our year and a half hop from mission to halfway house to Salvation Army shelter. My mother ended up applying for welfare checks and food stamps, which about six years ago provided us with the opportunity to rent a very small, cheap apartment around the corner from the mission we were staying in at the time.

We still live in that apartment today. My little sister is now ten years old and my mother has yet to find a job. These days I'm so busy trying to succeed in school that I don't really have time to stop and think about my past, but sometimes when I do think back to my childhood, I want to cry. I've changed so much that it's as though the little girl of my youth was someone else who I felt sorry for. I've grown up so differently than my friends, I feel that I completely missed out on a real childhood. If it weren't for my teachers, I would not be sitting here right now typing this paper. I would not be near where I am today if my teachers and friends throughout the years had not helped me the way they have.

I feel like my entire life has been a lesson given the hard way. Sometimes I still want to cry. I want someone else to feel sorry for that little girl that I knew so long ago. Then I remember how many people have helped me, how much I've been through in my eighteen years on this earth that some people never experience in a lifetime, and my old friend Determination returns stronger than ever.

Now when I see people who are hungry and are living on the streets, I want to cry and lash out at society. I want to scream at all the people who think their major problem is the lack of a pair of earrings to match their prom dresses. I want to take all the money that is given to already well-off people on game shows and hand it out to those people who have never had the luxury of owning a television. I want to smother the world with the cries of all the starving children in Ethiopia until society finally wakes up and realizes that our number one problem is not the deficit or the loss of a battleship, but instead homelessness and starvation of millions of our citizens.

I have been transformed from a shy girl who had no real knowledge of the world around her, to a young lady who knows what awaits her out there and who is going to use everything within her power to be a part of it, if it is worthwhile, and to change it, if it is not.

This is the Kathy who never missed a day of school, her broad, pleasant features well scrubbed, her shoulder-length dark blond hair neatly combed in spite of another night's sleep on a row of chairs in an apartment without running water. She and her old friend Determination were not content to simply get all the assignments done on time. They had to be done well, spiced with an extra bit of reading, an especially well written paper. Kathy was incensed that she had been deemed unqualified for the prestigious advanced placement English class. She would show up that faithless teacher by doing all the preparatory readings for the A.P. exam while keeping up with the reading for my course.

She could have written about her painting. From the day she turned it in as part of an assignment linked to a novel we were reading, her oil painting, an eighteen-by-thirty-inch canvas, became a classroom fixture in its perch in the chalk tray of my front blackboard. In it, a young girl of beatific expression kneels in the bushes by a riverbank, surrounded by supernatural apparitions in the air, in the luminous greenery, in the river water. Toward the end of the year, the canvas disappeared for a few days. Kathy reclaimed it to paint over the parts she felt were not right the first time and needed repair before it became a permanent gift.

Painting, writing, dancing—Kathy was drawn to all of them. Unlike so many people who grow up poor and spend their lives slaking their thirst for money, she thirsted for expression, for giving voice to the sheer exuberance of being alive.

Once a photographer visited our school to prepare the students for an exhibition of his work that they would see the following week. He did what more adults need to do for students: he told them his story. It was a fairy tale journey from poverty and school failure to the accidental discovery of the camera, which in turn carried him to assignments all over the world. For the past five years he had been photographing scenes in hospital emergency rooms, and now, in middle age, he had decided to become a doctor.

Kathy approached him after the talk. She waited patiently until her classmates were done. When she spoke it was with self-consciously averted eyes and with a voice straining to mask its passion.

"I loved your talk. I want to do *everything.*"

Kathy's life was not an unbroken triumphal march from the Greyhound station to the Halls of Ivy. Her male radar was flawed and often locked on young men unworthy of her attention. As a result, she risked the fate that brought her mother two children without benefit of even one legal husband. Her neediness put off even some of her good friends, who were sometimes bewildered by her ineptness at expressing simple gratitude for the considerable favors they were called upon to extend—money, rides, meals. She had a particularly painful falling out with a teacher whose family had virtually taken her in during her senior year. In return for baby-sitting services, he rescued her from her dungeon of an apartment for days at a time, bought her school clothes, ferried her to interviews. Then, over a violation of household rules, Kathy was banished under circumstances that didn't reflect well on either party.

For the most part, though, Kathy's grit and tenacity called forth from others the desire to support this incredible upward thrust, this reaching for the light. Her teachers put her forward as a candidate for a summer program in Israel after her junior year, her first experience in a world beyond Houston's grim Fifth Ward neighborhood. She had no trouble amassing the awed letters of recommendation that brought bouquets of scholarships and college acceptances. Another parent provided her with a stunning prom dress and all the fixings. In responding to Kathy's needs there was always the clear sense that one was sending good money after good.

Kathy is going to a prestigious women's college in New England that found her personal testimonial and her school record worthy of a full scholarship. There may be pitfalls ahead, but, like Doug's plants, Kathy has put strong roots down into rich soil, with a little help from friends, teachers, institutions, even from her father, who made a late reappearance in her life. But in the end, Kathy's refusal to be defeated by circumstances remains a blessed mystery, a rebuke to those of us inclined to succumb to the all too ready excuses for failure in ourselves and others.

CHAPTER *20*

Terence:
Voodoo Education

When Terence's letter of acceptance arrived from the University of Pennsylvania, he left a note on my desk. "See you in Philadelphia year after next, Doc." Like a good student of mathematics, he was extrapolating from the unusual numerical progression that represented our life together: Terence had been my student in the sixth, eighth, tenth, and twelfth grades. We had, in effect, graduated together from middle school when I moved to the same high school he had chosen at the end of his eighth-grade year. It began to seem as if we were bound together for life.

I would not mind the chance at a biennial check-in with him; a good story requires character development. Terence has shown plenty of that, and there's more to come. When he came to my classroom of precocious, driven sixth graders, Terence looked like a "project," as basketball coaches refer to draft picks with raw promise buried under layers of flaws and inexperience. There is always the implication that success is a long shot. He was undisciplined in thought and behavior, and he approached school as an adversary to be outsmarted. His mouth was set in a smirk that seemed to bespeak disdain—not angry defiance, but nonetheless a determination to go his own way. Terence was experimenting with the part of the bad little black boy who, despite his obvious gifts, was determined to snatch defeat from the jaws of victory.

And here is Terence seven years later looking back at me from the photo on my desk. His eyes are partly concealed behind a pair of brown shades. He is standing in the hallway of our high school outside the Spanish classroom with the obligatory Bienvenidos sign over the door. His arms are open wide in a sweeping gesture: this piece of the world I lay claim to. And there is about him a sense of entitlement that his classmates and his elders are inclined to see as arrogance: I am going to be heard from.

Somehow or other, that smirking, undisciplined boy has transformed himself into a tall, handsome young black man with a golden tongue. In his junior year I sponsored Terence for a scholarship being offered by a group of women business executives in Houston. From the twelfth floor of the elegant hotel in which the awards banquet was being held, the flat, surprisingly luxuriant green city stretched out for miles. Although these women had their own war stories to tell of their difficult climbs to even the lower echelons of power, there was a sense in the room of having arrived, of at least being close to the top, to the control tower from which the flow of commerce was regulated.

Terence was undaunted by his surroundings. He and his mother were the only blacks in the room, but they appeared to be more comfortable than I on this alien turf. We had been together long enough for me to guess that the familiar smirk masked an amusement at the carrying-on of these high-powered women: door prizes, drawings for stuffed animals and crockery, punctuated by game show shrieks; a hot line of congratulatory announcements about new positions, promotions, retirements. From time to time I flashed my best social critic's glance of disbelief in Terence's direction, but his response was more opaque. He was the dispassionate anthropologist, processing it all for future use.

The evening's keynote speaker was a Houston oil company executive—male—who is known in town as a leading business-community proponent of educational reform. This most mercantile of cities has spawned dozens of school-business "partnerships," born of a tangled mixture of genuine social concern and panic about the disastrous effects of an ill-educated workforce on business. The talk, lightly applauded, was a judicious mixture of education atrocity stories and exhortations to change.

On to the awards. The other student being honored, a Hispanic young lady caught in a scheduling crunch between the banquet and a school function, barely touched down long enough to utter her thank you in a quiet, diffident voice. Then her parents whisked her off to the next stop like a presidential candidate on the hustings.

Now it was Terence's turn. He ambled up to the microphone cool and loose, just enough street in his walk to remind the audience of who he was, but not enough to unnerve them with threatening ghetto visions. Instead of a lick and a promise thank you to match his predecessor's, Terence launched into a ten-minute monologue spellbinding in its flirtation with inappropriateness. It was a performance hard to reproduce on paper, more style than substance, delivered without a pause, without a moment's grasping for words. He was preacher, loner, and snake oil salesman in equal measure. Without breaking step Terence segued from an analysis of American society to his own personal philosophy of success to predictions about our country's role in the future international economy.

In the famous Battle Royal scene in Ralph Ellison's

Invisible Man, which Terence had read in my tenth grade class, the black boys entertain a local businessman's dinner by bashing each other into senselessness in a boxing ring while they're blindfolded, then scrambling for pennies on an electrified grid. The narrator has come to the degrading event in the mistaken belief that he is to deliver his award-winning speech on Booker T. Washington.

Terence was earning his pennies entirely with his words. No need for electric shock or self-humiliation. He was still entertaining the White Folk, but on his own terms, regaling them with stories of the black bankers and businessmen from whom he was gleaning wisdom that might inform his own future success. The women loved every minute of it. The hospital administrators, personnel department heads, and corporate public relations directors exchanged remarks about the bright future that awaited this smooth, articulate, most presentable young man.

Terence's classmates and I had seen many similar performances over the years. In school he delivered them from a cross-legged posture, slumped low in his chair, already the successful banker declaiming from behind an oversized executive desk. His audience greeted these displays with a mixture of amusement and fascination. He could be astute and penetrating, but just as often his words were pudding-smooth hokum. Once Terence delivered a five-minute discourse on a short story he had not read. Echoing the jazz music he loved so much, he was playing riffs on the story's title, which in this case was totally misleading. The class's laughter grew along with the hole Terence's obvious ignorance of the story was digging. After a while he stopped and smiled disarmingly, caught out but offering no apologies. These moments became rarer as we hopscotched together across the even-numbered grades, but they served as a constant reminder of the wisp that separates con man from crusader.

There is one detail in the photograph on my desk that I have been saving. Terence is wearing a pill-box-shaped hat of many colors—red, green, blue, orange—arranged in a crazy-quilt pattern of sharp-edged geometric forms. It is tilted slightly, its flat top slanted down to the right in the manner of the skewed, asymmetrical haircuts popular among my black male students these days. It is Terence's African statement. These assertions of his heritage—a hat, a loosely fitting multicolored shirt—are subtle, calculatingly underdone. Unlike his heritage-conscious precursors in the late sixties and early seventies, he felt no need to be seen only in dashiki. He was comfortable with his blackness, without the need for excessive props to serve as cue cards for his identity.

Terence's people, like so many other black families in Houston, had come to the big city from rural Louisiana. New Orleans may have seemed a more logical destination, but without an industrial base it had little to offer the migrants. They brought to the city an unusually rich Creole culture— a unique mix of French, Cajun, black, and Indian elements reflected in its zydeco music, its cooking, its lilting speech laced with French expressions and interjections. Centuries of commerce among the diverse groups had produced a population of extraordinary hybrid vigor, ranging in appearance from pale and blue-eyed to night black.

And here are enduring families whose strength belies the prevailing sociological rhetoric about the dissolution of the black family. Terence has returned often to Louisiana for the reunion of the Marcelous clan, a mammoth event that draws many hundreds of family members, who return from different places to reaffirm their ties to each other and to their home territory. The Creoles, like the Mexicans and Puerto Ricans, are blessed among migrating populations in their ability to shuttle freely between the old world and the new, never having to forsake their roots entirely.

So Terence and some of his Creole classmates could bring into our discussions a living culture they had experienced back "home" in its original habitat. He could match Maxine Hong Kingston superstition for superstition with tales from the bayous and backwaters. His relatives told him their experiences with the Fi-Fo-Lay, the spirit of dead babies that haunts the murky places in the form of a glowing light hunters mistake for the lantern they set on their porches to guide them home at night. When they seek to follow that light it migrates deeper into the swamp's recesses. Once they have been totally led astray it emits an eerie, mocking laughter before it departs, leaving them to find their own way home.

A bridge in his family's town was said to be haunted by spirits whose presence dogs could sense. They refused to cross that bridge, no matter what enticements or punishments their masters were meting out. A skeptical Terence set up a good, rational man-of-science test. Controlling for factors of conditioning and inadvertently signaled human expectations, he brought a dog from elsewhere and turned to coax it across himself—with the same lack of success. He challenged the class to "Draw your own conclusions."

Creole culture is laced with strands of voodoo. Terence had educated himself in its history and practice and regaled the class with a rich gumbo of sex orgies, initiation rites, hexes, and healings. In his most silky, believe-it-or-not tone, he delivered a story of a young man who had wronged his sister and had broken both his legs in an automobile accident on the day she hexed him. For Terence, these strange, unaccountable powers were also part of his legacy.

Everything about Terence—his strong sense of self and entitlement, his ambitious striving—was rooted in what his culture and his family had bestowed on him. And he had built outward from that parochial base in the Louisiana swamps toward a broader, more universal appreciation of his black roots. Unlike most of his contemporaries, he favored jazz over contemporary soul and rap. I remember my surprise in discovering that the black students in a Mississippi college where I taught in the sixties knew nothing of jazz or blues. Imagine the irony of a New York Jew introducing those students to perhaps the greatest cultural contribution of their people. The shoe was on the other foot with Terence, who often brought in recordings from his collection to play as background music during our class journal-writing time. The day after he played Dexter Gordon for us, I was off to Sound Warehouse in search of my own copy.

Terence knew his black history, from the ideological disputes of the earlier part of the century to the more recent civil rights struggles. And he felt obligated to share his knowledge with other black students, a secular soul saver, spreading the gospel. He was president of a predominantly black quasi-fraternity on campus called the Young Gents, about which we clashed several times. I had little tolerance for their humiliating and degrading initiation rites. Was there no better way to bind people to a group, to create love and loyalty? Spike Lee has captured it all in *School Daze*—the initiation on all fours, bound in neck chains, pretending to be dogs, the rituals that stress conformity in dress, line marches complete with canes wielded with lockstep precision worthy of the Rockettes.

Terence added a new dimension to the activities of the Young Gents that tempered my criticism of the group and their right to exist on a campus where fraternities were banned. He had his troops posting signs in the otherwise grimly bare hallways, our equivalent of the once adless vistas of gray Soviet cities. Our students were being introduced to the words of Marcus Garvey, W. E. B. Du Bois, Frederick Douglass. Whether they took any more note of the placards than they do of their teachers' carefully designed bulletin boards, the signmakers themselves were being educated. The Young Gents and their female counterparts, the Ladies of Sophistication, distributed flyers with information of cultural interest to black students. Most of the Young Gents were students in the school's Vanguard program for gifted students. The posters and handouts were an attempt to reach across that gap to speak directly to the "regulars" who had little exposure to anything beyond M. C. Hammer and the latest crop of rappers. Terence had even begun to seek out the regular students in the school's interstices where they slipped off to drink and gab while cutting classes. He was determined to convince them that they were committing suicide by not attending class, a message far more potent from the mouth of a fellow student than from the assistant principal, whose sermons were so predictable you could lip-synch them.

For his trouble, Terence was branded a racist by some whites for addressing his message to an exclusively black audience. Patiently, Terence tried to explain to his white classmates and teachers that he intended no racial slight in his campaign. He was simply targeting the audience most in need of hearing it, those most "at risk," in the jargon of the day.

Terence's voodoo-wielding sister had been acting in and writing plays since her high school days and was now in New York pursuing that cruelest of professions. Although he had no intention of following such an unremunerative path, Terence had the family gift for theater. In his senior year he directed and performed in one of the most memorable student performances ever seen in my classroom. His troupe of four wove together poetry, music, and original drama around the theme "Black Protest in the Sixties." I knew from the number of weekend preparation dates being negotiated that something special was evolving, and for once I had the foresight to record it on video. Now Terence is with me permanently as civil rights worker, as Black Panther spewing revolutionary rhetoric correct down to the smallest inflection, as returning Vietnam vet, broken and bitter. How had he succeeded in breathing life into these ghosts who had crossed the stage of history before he was born? It was an uncanny performance and contained within it the secret of Terence's self-assurance. The blackness that weighed down so many others was his source of uplift. It salved the wounds of his parents' bitter divorce in his early teen years, which might have driven other kids to the streets and drugs. Terence got by because, in the largest sense, he knew who he was. And it was good.

All through high school Terence was announcing to the world that he was headed for a black college. It seemed the logical extension of his beliefs about race, culture, and identity. He favored Xavier U in New Orleans, a perfect synthesis of his family history in Louisiana, his jazz interests, and his search for a congenial black environment. Xavier had achieved some national attention for its success in preparing black students for careers in science and medicine, and although these were not Terence's interests, they bespoke an academic program of some quality.

Then came the Penn acceptance with the scholarship offer larger than the annual salary Terence's mother earns as a secretary-receptionist in the school district office. His good fortune left him with a difficult, albeit enviable, choice. Toward what flavor college did he incline, black or white?

The media have reported a significant turnaround in college selection patterns by black students. An increasing number are voluntarily enrolling in the black colleges that were their parents' only choice in the era of segregation. At Tougaloo College in Mississippi in 1965 I taught a broad range of black students who had been forced together by a hostile society. When the doors of white institutions opened to blacks, the best and the brightest were skimmed off by prestigious colleges eager to make their quota of minority students. This trend threatened to relegate black colleges to the permanent role of remedial institution, repositories of students not equipped to compete in more demanding schools.

The black colleges' recent return to favor is fueled by a complicated combination of circumstances. In spite of conservative outcries about preferential treatment for minorities, the Reagan years brought sharp cutbacks in federal scholarship aid. Many of my bright black students are still much in demand at white schools, which accept them but often don't offer sufficient support to make it possible for them to attend. The black colleges they choose instead are more affordable. Second, the story of black students in white colleges over the past decade and more has not been an uplifting one. Blacks have been subject to overt racism—cross burnings, scrawled racial slurs, bigoted campus media broadcasts— and to more subtle institutional racism reflected in unrepresentative curriculum offerings and hiring policies that kept the number of black faces on campus at a minimum. Many good people are earnestly working to remedy these problems, but meanwhile a liberal, integrationist child of the sixties can only be saddened by the backward steps we are taking toward a division into separate, mutually uncomprehending societies. In this regard, the campuses only reflect the growing distance between black and white. We rarely live, work, or study together, and when we do it is like the parallel play of young children who may occupy the same space but seldom turn toward one another for a shared moment.

The students in my high school classes for the gifted constitute one of those rare enclaves where integration works—

more or less. Although the races tend to go their own way at lunch, after school, for extracurricular activities, they work together comfortably on academic tasks, laugh together, and enjoy and respect their differences. So when Tiffany and Deshaunda and Pete choose Prairie View A&M or Morgan State or Florida A&M over Tulane and Amherst and the University of Texas, it feels as if all of us are taking a giant step backward. I understand their decisions, but I worry that they will never even know what they might be missing in quality of teaching or in exposure to diverse ideas. And I regret the loss to the white students who will never experience the richness of their language, their family stories, the unique black perspective on the world. They will be comfortable and happy in their black schools and there are things they will get from living among their own kind that will strengthen them in ways that perhaps are not possible in "white" schools. I like to think of it as a transitional period for all of us, a time of strengthening identities that will allow us to meet later as real equals, free of the racial baggage that stands between us. But I worry that the habits of separation will cut deep grooves, ruts from which we will no longer be able to extricate ourselves.

Terence chose Penn after some soul-searching, and he will not be uncomfortable there. Because his identity is firmly in place, he will move without threat in a world that some of his black classmates might still find intimidating. In an interview with a Houston newspaper reporter, Terence announced that he had decided it was okay to choose Penn over a black college because he was clear about his long-term goals: to become an investment banker, to get rich, and to bring that money back to the black community where he can put it to use for the greater good. Going to a white school was not an abandonment of his principles, just a more effective way of attaining them. His words might be spiced with a touch of jive, but I've seen enough of Terence's transformation from smart-ass to focused senior class president to leave me hopeful. On the other hand, the road to Philadelphia is, as they say, paved with good intentions.

The odds are that Terence and I won't manage to keep our rendezvous up north. I'll see him again during one of those hit-and-run visits graduates like to make during their freshman-year breaks, a sincere though usually doomed attempt to reinfuse old relationships with a semblance of their former energy. In fact they serve to confirm for students that indeed they have outgrown the world of their earlier triumphs and it's best to face forward and not dwell too much on a past that looks like the view through the wrong end of a telescope.

So I'll have to make do with the memory of my final encounter with Terence and his family. It is graduation day at Jones. The ceremony has taken place at the elegant concert hall downtown that bears the name of the same oil-rich benefactor our school is named for. The band has played; the chorus has sung; the platform guests have been introduced; the valedictorian has heeded my exhortation to say something personal, to eschew the traditional cliché-riddled speech in which the words roll by, as Garrison Keillor describes them, "like empty boxcars"; the seniors have walked across the stage for their diplomas; a few have bugalooed or shimmied or raised their arms in victorious postures to distinguish themselves from the masses.

Now, on the oppressive summer sidewalk outside Jones Hall, graduates are stripping off their gold graduation gowns and heading for an afternoon of celebration—restaurant lunches, parties, family gatherings. Terence's mother has invited me to a reception in his honor at a small restaurant/ catering hall on the edge of downtown. It is the only building in all of Houston that looks like a transplant from New

Orleans's French Quarter or Garden District—an interior courtyard, welded metal railings. Inside, cool jazz is being piped over the loudspeaker, music that only Terence himself could have chosen for the occasion. Mrs. Marcelous takes my wife and me on a tour of the tables to meet Terence's extraordinarily multicolored Creole family. On a table, a shrine to the graduate has been erected. The baby pictures, school pictures, letters of acceptance are signposts of success without a hint of the sadness and setbacks that are the stuff of real life. Where is Daddy?

Terence works the room like a successful politician, shaking hands, making sure everyone is happy. Periodically he sinks down at a table full of friends to let his hair down and chill a while. We eat from the buffet, we sample the graduation cake and rise to say good-bye to Terence and his mother before we move on to another party. As we leave Terence is surrounded by his family, his friends, his music, his history. They will see him through whatever comes next.

CHAPTER 21

Carlotta: She's Leaving Home

Carlotta is a girl I would have been quick to fall in love with when I was seventeen. She is beautiful in that pure, clear way that carries the promise of deep, intense relationship, not backseat sex. In her first day in my class, she responded to my suggestion that students write about their names by expressing her preference for hearing hers pronounced with the rolling *r* of her Hispanic heritage rather than its flat American counterpart. Thus she was announcing simultaneously that, in the largest sense, she wanted people to respond to who she was, and that she was sensitive to even the smallest of aesthetic issues.

Carlotta's wide, curious eyes fix on you from within a surrounding sea of deeply tinted freckles. Until a drastic shift to a pixie-short haircut late in the year, she alternated between a youthful ponytail and a beret under which even loose hair disappeared, a hint of romantic visions of lives awaiting her beyond Houston.

When we discuss literature in class, it is Carlotta whose modest, thoughtful comments penetrate closest to the heart of the piece. She speaks in a soft, melodious voice, virtually without a trace of the accent that continues to flavor the speech of most of her Hispanic classmates. As she speaks, broad smiles overtake her features in bursts that even seem to surprise her. Students lean forward to hear her, confident that her words, drawn up out of deep wellsprings of sensitivity, will justify the effort.

As early as October of her senior year, Carlotta was wrestling with her college choices in terms that became the year's leitmotivs. In her journals she recorded idyllic fantasies of trudging through the fallen leaves of a mythic New England picture-book campus this time next year. It happens that one of my regular routes through town takes me past Carolotta's street. From the interstate, an exit or two short of the functional ugliness of the Houston Ship Channel with its oil storage tanks, loading cranes, and refinery stacks, I can see her house. Her father's moving trucks, with the family name emblazoned in big block letters on the sides, are parked alongside it. The house itself is neat and well painted, but not far off are warehouses and some of the most dilapidated housing stock anywhere in the city. Nothing could be farther from that picture-book campus.

But there is also anguish in the journal. One entry she invited me to read was written entirely in French. Fortunately, enough of my own high school French was intact to allow me to grasp that Carlotta was racked with guilt over the thought of leaving home. She loved her family so much, felt such closeness to them. How could she place herself two thousand miles away, to return only for scattered holidays?

I invited Carlotta in to talk about college, and she accepted my invitation for lunch the following day. It was a ponytail day. She came dressed in loose-fitting jeans and blouse. Carlotta was too self-conscious for form-fitting clothes that broadcast her sexuality.

"Dr. H"—she began virtually every sentence this way,

addressing me by title and name, which I took as a touching combination of respect and affection—"I'm so confused I can hardly get out of bed in the morning."

"Tell me what the pluses and minuses are for each choice, Carlotta." I always hope that this toting-up process will reveal to the choicemaker that one option weighs in more heavily than the other.

"If I go, Dr. H, I leave my mother when she needs me." Her parents' marriage was crumbling. Like so many of her classmates, Carlotta was discovering that she was the glue that held her family together. Remove her and much of the precarious structure was in danger of collapse.

"And what about my sister? What would she do, Dr. H?" Angela, several years younger, was messing up in school and hanging out with the wrong people. Carlotta had that oldest child's sense of responsibility for keeping everything on track.

"And if you don't go, you'll never forgive yourself."

"That's right, Dr. H. I'll spend the rest of my life wondering what I had missed and how my life would have been different if I had gotten out of the Fifth Ward." Her face was showing that anguished intensity of someone tormented by a critical decision who is also relishing the sense of being oh so alive at this moment of choice.

"And if I apply and get in, Dr. H, how will I know if I made it on my own? I don't even want to check the box that says 'Hispanic' on the application." In truth, Carlotta's SAT scores were not impressive. I have never succeeded in penetrating the mystery of how poorly those scores reflect the true ability of students like Carlotta, a thoughtful writer and one of the best literary analysts I had taught. I knew from experience with students before her that she would do just fine once she was past the gatekeepers, but she would never get past them unless she agreed to check that minority box on the application.

"Look, Carlotta, you've got to take advantage of every leg up that's available to you. You have no idea what hidden advantages other students bring with them. Do you know what a legacy is? Do you realize that not-so-great students get into these schools because someone in their families went there? That could never happen in your family."

In the little time that was left in the truncated lunch period, I urged her to go ahead and at least finish applying; then, if the choice became hers, she could worry about the actual decision later.

The first three months of the new year are an odd period of limbo for college-bound seniors. Applications are in, no prospect of news is on the immediate horizon, and there is a business-as-usual air about school that belies the fact that seismic forces are gathering below the surface.

In April the earth began to shift. First, Carlotta failed to get into the most prestigious local university to which she had applied, thus eliminating the most desirable close-to-home option, a shot at campus life within a Metro bus ride of the nest. Shortly thereafter came the letter of acceptance from a well-known women's college in New England, the embodiment of Carlotta's autumn leaves fantasy. The school offered her a large scholarship, but the family would still have to supplement it with several thousand dollars of its own. Not out of the question, given her father's moving trucks, but definitely more of a strain on the family than going to the local commuter college.

But the real issue was not financial. All of Carlotta's earlier conflicts about leaving home resurfaced, along with some new wrinkles. How could she manage on her own— she who had never even done her own laundry? How could she leave her community? These were all the doubts with which she laced her comments during another round of our patented lunchtime soul-searchings, arranged by Kathy, who had been accepted to the same school and was distressed that Carlotta's position against going was hardening. She pleaded with me to see her, fearful that Carlotta would never be able to forgive herself later for passing up an opportunity to change her life that would not come again.

At home Carlotta was being met with a resigned silence from her mother and a subtle, complex brand of resistance from her father. He had chosen not to forbid her to go. He would not stand in her way if she chose to go, nor would he drive her out of the family. But he made it clear that he expected the worst. The daughter of a family friend had gone off to college and had returned pregnant, bringing disgrace on herself and her family. This is what awaited Hispanic girls who strayed from home. This softer, guilt-style assault was much harder for Carlotta to withstand than any flat-out, stiff-necked prohibition. Still, after weeks of agonizing, she informed me, almost by the way, heading for lunch at the end of our English class, "I decided to go." Almost immediately the oppressive brooding was gone and in a few days the New Carlotta of the pixie haircut appeared, shorn of the longer hair of her prom photo, teased and sprayed into calculated Latin disarray.

I rejoiced in Carlotta's decision, the victory of the forces of light over the forces of darkness, savored vicariously all the discoveries, large and small, that are going to reshape Carlotta on that idyllic New England campus. But with her departure I was beset by my own doubts.

My daughters, too, were leaving home. It seems oddly unjust to be thus rewarded for all those years of building a loving, caring family in which people really *do* sit down to dinner together every night and look forward to rehashing the day's events. A student of mine, a veteran of years of hit-and-run meals in her single-parent family, described a sleep-over experience at a friend's, complete with family dinner, "straight out of Beaver Cleaver. I could barely keep from laughing." That scene could have been filmed at our house; it was the vision of the empty chair at the dinner table that loosed those expensive tears. The stronger the bonds, the more painful and unfair the parting.

We have come to see the passage out of the nest as an inevitability, the cost of doing business in a mobile society. In any given middle-class family the odds are high that the three living generations are linked not by shared Sunday dinners but by phone cards and frequent-flyer coupons. In our family, there are children in California and Michigan, parents in Texas, and grandparents in Florida, with other siblings sprinkled through Illinois and New York, the original nests from which this dispersal began.

In America we are torn between two conflicting ideal visions of relations between self and community. On the one hand there is the breakaway experience that reaches back simultaneously to the core of our pioneering and immigrant heritages to glorify the individual setting off alone to make a mark on the world. If old bonds must be severed in the process, so be it. Our hero embraces parents, friends, lovers before venturing forth on the journey; they may never see each other again. News of eventual successes will arrive in scattered letters and thirdhand reports.

The contrasting vision is that of the beloved community in which each individual owns a membership in perpetuity. The ties to family and friends are permanent, deepening with the shared events of growing and aging, of birth, marriage, tragedy, and death. It is the small town idyll both of *Our Town* America and of the seamless life of the peasant village left behind in the old world for the flight to America. Once my daughter asked wistfully why we couldn't all return to the days of the shtetl when families could expect to live side by side as the generations unrolled like the sewn sections of a Torah scroll. Then she waved good-bye and boarded the plane to return to her tiny, overpriced apartment in San Francisco.

Each of these versions of contemporary life carries its own destructive virus, which drives us to its opposite in search of a cure. The individual on that solitary quest for success is beset by loneliness, isolation, a loss of meaning resulting from confusion about his or her place in the world. The seeker after the nurturing womblike community faces a smothering sameness, a proximity that breeds rancor. Those families and friends enclosed within the shtetl generation after generation bickered, gossiped, intruded; there was no shade in which the individual spirit could seek shelter.

I find myself less and less able to pass judgment on which way lies greater happiness—in breaking the gravitational pull and moving off toward the outer reaches of uncharted experience or in giving in to, even exulting in, the pull back to the safe, familiar, warm center. Is Carlotta in the process of giving up her amniotic sustenance or is she throwing off her restraining shackles? Each metaphor seems to come from a different universe.

We still subscribe to the newspaper published in the small town we left for Houston so many years ago. Every June an issue arrives with the high school graduation supplement tucked into its pages. It contains an individual yearbook-size photo of each graduate, under which is inscribed that student's postgraduate plans and anticipated major if the plan calls for college: TAMMY JOHNSON, KEENE STATE COLLEGE, PHYSICAL THERAPY; MARK BLANCHETTE, DELAYED COLLEGE, TRAVEL; JENNIFER FOOTE, MANAGEMENT TRAINEE, AMES DEPARTMENT STORE; MICHAEL COLE, POMONA COLLEGE, POLITICAL SCIENCE.

As we scan the photos, we cheer on the Michaels who are

headed off to distant "good" schools. They are the victors, the success stories. We groan a bit over the Tammys, who, although they're en route to college, have made a mediocre choice that will keep them close to home. The Marks and the Jennifers are the defeats. He will return from his travels and settle in to work at the local lumber company, and she will never leave the small-town world, intellectually or physically. Three years from now, on my annual summer return visit, I will meet her at the local supermarket, her baby's feet dangling through the appointed stockade slots at the back of the shopping cart.

At the end of this scorekeeping exercise we stop, overtaken by our arrogance. By what right have we become the arbiters of happiness? It is not at all clear which of these lives is headed toward fulfillment and which toward confusion. Those who have stayed in our small town close to friends, their children's grandparents just up the road, seem content. There is work. The air is good and the landscape is pleasing to the eye. Loneliness, confusion, and failure or, even with "success," a more profound dislocation may await them at Oberlin or Pomona.

As with everything else in life, there are trade-offs. Whichever of the myths Carlotta buys into will carry its own costly price tag.

PART FIVE

Postscript:
New Show in Town

The auditorium of Lamar High School is full right up to the balcony seats. So many parents have turned out to hear about the new school that we've had to promise to lay on a second shift to accommodate the people who are still waiting outside. After almost three years of planning, we've been taking our show on the road in a series of community meetings like this one to explain the vision and philosophy of the new school on which Rice University and the Houston Independent School District have been collaborating. For me, it is time stolen from my work at Jones, evenings away from the stacks of ungraded papers that haunt me relentlessly.

Although this crowd is predominantly white, the meetings in black and Hispanic parts of town have also been well attended. There is a tremendous hunger for decent public education that crosses racial, ethnic, and class lines. I know from a number of individual conversations that the hunger is particularly intense among parents of middle schoolers who are concerned in equal measure for their kids' safety and their education. It's painful to acknowledge our failure to provide more options that meet even the modest standards of most parents.

The centerpiece of the rally—more like a tent revival than an informational meeting—is a talk by the school's principal, whom everyone refers to simply as Kay; she will lay out the basic philosophy and vision of the school and explain the application process.

Other speakers have already explained the history and evolution of the school. The school board approved a hefty budget to create a school to serve a dual function as both overflow facility to relieve overcrowding in the well-to-do West University community and as "professional development school" that embodies models of good practice for new teachers and experienced practitioners throughout the district.

The physical plans that evolved out of a long series of meetings among the architects, school district administrators, university people, parents, and teachers are spectacular. Kay had the scale model set up in the lobby where people could inspect the unique pod design: clusters of five classrooms, each sprouting from a central spine that housed the shared communal spaces—auditorium, cafeteria, and gym. The vaulted library occupies the physical and symbolic heart of the structure.

Once the physical design was established and construction begun, an ever-widening circle of planners explored what kind of learning world should be created within these walls. The original six from Rice and the school district grew to sixteen with the addition of teachers, administrators, and community representatives, then into the hundreds with the creation of task forces to study governance, curriculum, parent and community involvement, student enrollment and assessment. It was a heady time as educational consultants from all over the country were invited to planning conferences to share their experiences with similar ventures on their visits to schools that had managed to transform themselves from educational wastelands into successful learning communities.

There were warnings. "Keep it small," said Michelle Fine of the Philadelphia Schools Collaborative. "Build in sufficient time for teachers to plan and collaborate," advised Jay and Helen Featherstone of Michigan State University. Lucy Matos of Central Park East in New York exhorted us to anchor our school firmly in the community. Finally, David Cohen, a wise and wary friend from the University of Michigan, left us with these ominous words: "I wish you luck. Ventures like this rarely succeed."

Kay is presenting to her hungry audience a distillation of this long planning process. None of the central tenets she is laying out in her homespun East Texas drawl is unique in its own right, but rarely have they been brought together in one package. First, she explained, in an increasingly multicultural city like Houston, it is the school's responsibility to prepare children to live in more than one world. Therefore the program will be dual-language—instruction in Spanish and English—with the goal that every student will emerge from this kindergarten to eighth grade school fluent in both languages.

Second, the classrooms in each cluster will be multiage rather than the traditional single-graded rooms. In fancy contemporary garb, we were re-creating the world of the one-room school where a community of students functioned more like a family of siblings, assisting and supporting one another and allowing opportunities for students to slide up and down the developmental and cognitive ladder as subject

255

matter and emotional state required. Most important, the multigrade classrooms would provide a continuity and stability lacking in so many children's lives by keeping them in the same "family" across three-year stretches.

"Now, y'all remember your own time in school. It was probably a whole lot of desk work out of textbooks, taking notes, and copying stuff off the blackboard. We think that kids learn best when they're active—doing things, working on projects, working in groups. Instead of reading a chapter in the textbooks about an Indian tribe, they might build a whole Indian village, write legends for the tribe, figuring out how much corn they'd need to plant to feed everyone. That way they'd also be combining a bunch of different subject areas—social studies, English, math, science, art, music."

Without having to resort to educational jargon or invoking names from the educational pantheon, Kay has communicated a Deweyan vision of project-based, experiential learning from which tangible, meaningful products emerge and where writing—to take a more singular example—serves a real expressive or active purpose. To use Piaget's terms, children construct their own knowledge rather than having it delivered to them pre-chewed. The traditional disciplinary distinctions—English, math, social studies, science—would no longer prevail, replaced by a sense of the wholeness and connectedness of real learning. And children would be pursuing knowledge not in isolation from each other but as collaborators, which is after all what the management folks tell us they can expect in that mysterious territory known as the workplace.

It's a heady philosophy of learning, one that has been mud-wrestling for nearly a century now with a more four-square model of knowledge imparted by adult authorities to informed minds in need of the solid foundation from which independent learning and thinking can grow later. Just when one philosophy seems to be prevailing, there's a flip and the other sits astride its opponent.

Although I resonate strongly with this vision of active, collaborative learning, I suspect that most of the parents in the audience are more taken by the next portion of Kay's presentation about the role technology will play in the new school. The building is being wired to accommodate every technological advance that can be anticipated, including fiber optics and computer networking. There is applause when she announces that Compaq, a locally based computer giant, has pledged a computer for virtually every one of the school's twelve hundred students over the next several years. Rice, which has a national reputation for its work in computer science, will play a major support role in this area, training the school staff and linking the school's computers to its own, as well as to computers in other schools around the state.

I confess to Luddite leanings. Technological solutions to human problems leave me cold, although friends have made convincing cases for how even Shakespeare can be brought to life for students on CD-ROM in ways that are beyond the reach of all but a few gifted teachers. I am a tangle of inconsistencies on the subject, since I am also incensed on behalf of my Jones High School students over their limited access to the computer marvels that their suburban peers are exploring, thereby widening by the minute a gap that will surely rend our country in two if it continues.

In any case, I am not as awestruck as Kay's audience by this prospect of the electronic education awaiting the children in our as yet unnamed new school. For me, keyboards don't begin to address the issues of community and human relationships that are really at the root of meaningful learning. Kay's presentation is heavily laced with metaphoric references to family and "circles of friends," which appear to issue from a different universe than the worlds of information accessing and computer networking.

Standing behind Kay, waiting to be introduced by her, are two parents, both African-American, who have been part of the school planning process since the Parent/Community Relations Task Force was born. The presence of C. J. and Linda excites me as much as anything about the new school. Not only do they represent the diversity that vitalizes any community, they articulate with conviction some of my most deeply held beliefs, dating back to my days in Head Start, about how a school must be embedded in, not isolated from, its surroundings. I have heard them at earlier public meetings so I know that they will speak of using the human and physical resources of the community to enrich children's learning. They will talk of bringing social services into the building to help clear away obstacles in children's lives that distract from learning. Above all else, parents who have found the school a forbidding fortress to enter will be made to feel welcome. If they do, then children will benefit by feeling more at home, more like stakeholders than visitors.

Although Kay will not dwell on this subject in the public forum, talk about a democratic community—visions of a structure in which teachers, parents, and students participate in decision making at all levels of the school—percolated through the planning meetings. All three groups have been disenfranchised in different ways, and the vision of a teacher-directed school in which parents play important decision-making roles on the school's governing body and in which students resolve their own problems through mediation and conflict resolution is invigorating.

At the end of Kay's talk there is a rush for application forms, as there had been at the previous sessions. By the time the cycle of six community meetings is over, we will have in hand applications from more than seven thousand families, representing at least fifteen thousand children in all—probably 10 percent of all the kindergarten through eighth grade children in the school district. Each of those families absorbed a different piece of Kay's presentation and chose to ignore others that were either incomprehensible or irrelevant. Perhaps many already recognized more clearly than the planners that much of the rhetoric would inevitably drop away as the school bucked up against the constraints of bureaucratic inertia, urban racial politics, budgetary insufficiencies, and human frailties. But the number of applicants was testimony to the need for more choices for parents and children, accessible to poor and rich alike.

There were already structural flaws that would dog the school from the outset. The most obvious was the school's size. Twelve hundred children is just too many under one roof. I once heard a wise educator say, "Up to a certain size a school is a community. Beyond that it is an institution." Despite the mitigating structure of the five-classroom clusters, this school had exceeded the limits of community, which Deborah Meier of Central Park East contends is four hundred. As is so often the case, the reasons for the school's size are political and economic, not pedagogical—economies of scale, a need to demonstrate to budget-conscious school board members that their sizable outlay is serving significant numbers. Every new school and every attempt to reform an existing school begins with its own unique set of constraints and compromises that have the potential for vitiating the good it represents, but there is also the excitement and the urgency that grow from the belief that there is a better way, that schools can be richer, happier places for children, teachers, and parents, that there are already many things we know that work, if only we had the will and the commitment to implement them.

Time passes. Many of the students I have written about here have already graduated from college. The new school has been open for a year. For both there are stories to be told about dreams fulfilled and dreams deferred. Carlotta's father won twenty-seven million dollars in the lottery while she was off studying in France. Terence is on his way to law school. Kathy is teaching dance. Deborah still hasn't made it to college but has a good job and is living on her own. Arthur has disappeared. Kay, our principal, lasted only half the year in the new school before being promoted to a superintendency. The year was marked by enough institutional mood swings to qualify for a diagnosis of bipolar disorder. But these are all stories for another book.

We hear a lot about systemic change these days. I have tended to paint on smaller canvases—individual children, single classrooms, single schools. I know that, failing to increase the scale of change, we are doomed to create what Michelle Fine calls "precious moments" in education, shooting stars that barely illuminate the surrounding landscape before they flicker out. But one by one by one is all I really know how to do and, in the end, all I really believe in as a route to enduring change, and even that is open to question. The world's just too ornery and complicated for monolithic solutions, but we persist in searching for that gold-creating alchemist's formula anyway.

Yet even in the face of wracking doubts about the possibilities for change, we must act as if change is within reach, lest our children inherit from us a paralyzing pessimism and resignation that ensure that no change will occur. Against tremendous obstacles, it is up to us to, at the very least, emulate the heartening resilience of so many of our most courageous students.

Marvin Hoffman was born in Brooklyn and studied at the City College of New York. Since receiving a Ph.D. in clinical psychology from Harvard University, he has taught at every level from preschool to graduate school. He has been director of Teachers and Writers Collaborative in New York; associate director of the Child Development Group of Mississippi, one of the nation's first Head Start programs; director of graduate teacher education at Antioch/New England; and teaching principal in Bennington, New Hampshire. For the last fourteen years he has taught in Houston where he is on the faculties of Jones High School and Rice University. Currently he is on leave at the University of Chicago's Center for School Improvement. He is married to the novelist Rosellen Brown.

Interior design by Will Powers. Typeset in Slimbach and Rotis types by Stanton Publication Services, Inc. Printed on acid-free 55# Glatfelter paper by Edwards Brothers, Inc.

More nonfiction from Milkweed Editions:

Changing the Bully Who Rules the World:
Reading and Thinking about Ethics
Carol Bly

The Passionate, Accurate Story:
Making Your Heart's Truth into Literature
Carol Bly

Transforming a Rape Culture
Edited by Emilie Buchwald, Pamela Fletcher,
and Martha Roth

Rooms in the House of Stone
Michael Dorris

Grass Roots:
The Universe of Home
Paul Gruchow

The Mythic Family
Judith Guest

The Art of Writing:
Lu Chi's Wen Fu
Translated from the Chinese by Sam Hamill

Coming Home Crazy:
An Alphabet of China Essays
Bill Holm